Michael Huber

Ni
F-401

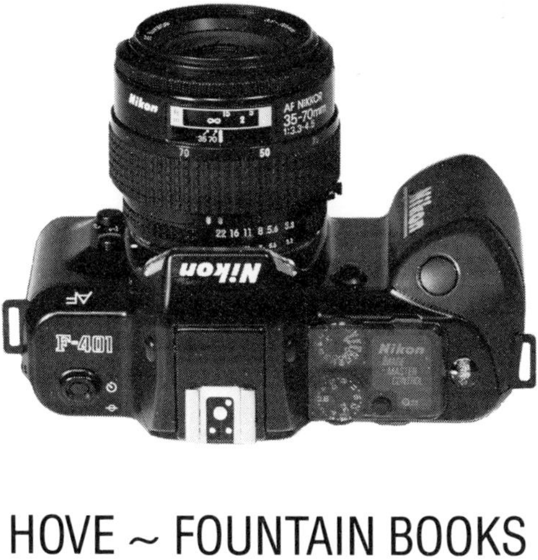

HOVE ~ FOUNTAIN BOOKS

In U.S.A. and Canada

the Nikon F-401 is known as the

NIKON N4004

All text, illustrations and data apply to cameras with either name

U.S. Edition ISBN 0-86343-150-X

NIKON F-401

First English Edition October 1988
English Translation from the original German
by Liselotte Sperl
Edited by George Wakefield
Series Editor Dennis Laney
Typeset by Alphabet Workshop, Eastbourne
Printed in Great Britain by
Purnell Book Production Ltd

ISBN 0 86343-145-3

Published by
HOVE FOUNTAIN BOOKS
the joint imprint of
Fountain Press Ltd & Hove Foto Books

45 The Broadway	34 Church Road
Tolworth	Hove
Surrey KT6 7DW	Sussex BN3 2GJ

U.K. Trade Distribution by
Fountain Press Ltd

Michael Huber · Nikon F-401

Contents

One Camera Suitable for Everyone

The recent success of autofocus SLR cameras could not be ignored by a major manufacturer such as Nikon. After introducing the F-501, which was aimed at the ambitious amateur photographer, Nikon followed with the F-401, which has similar features, but offers easier handling.

This model is the ideal tool for the newcomer to SLR photography. However, even the more ambitious SLR photographer will find it valuable as a second camera body with AF facility. The Image Master Control system of the F-401 combines automatic control of exposure, focusing and flash, making an incorrect exposure almost impossible.

Some of you may look down on such a fool-proof camera. But all its facilities demonstrate the advantages of modern technology: the photographer can concentrate fully on the subject without having to fiddle with all kinds of adjustments with knobs and buttons. Even so, it will be necessary to acquaint yourself with this camera and it is my task to introduce you to all its functions in order to reduce initial failures to a minimum. Once you have started using it you will see that there is more behind its smooth exterior than meets the eye.

This book has been arranged so that the beginning of each chapter summarizes the most important points for handling the camera, i.e.: what button do I have to press, so that...

There then follows a description of the types of subjects and the shooting situations best suited for the techniques described in that chapter. The following chapters deal with any technical or photographic limitations, and when it may be better to use a different shooting mode. The last chapters are devoted to the technical details. The latter will be of interest to those with a techical inclination, but will also provide useful information for the ambitious photographer who is interested in understanding his equipment.

Operating Functions

The successful photographer can handle his camera automatically. We shall therefore start by looking at the operating elements in detail.

Looking at the camera from the top with the lens pointing forward, we see on the right, on the bulging handgrip, the shutter release button. This is a multi-function control: it serves as the switch for exposure control and autofocusing, as the release for the shutter, and as the trigger for motorized film advance. Depressing the release lightly to fingerguard level activates the exposure meter and the autofocus system when the red exposure LED, as well as the green autofocus LED, will light up at the bottom of the viewfinder. This means that the exposure control will take a reading which will be used to set the aperture and shutter speed, and the autofocus function takes a distance reading, which is used by the autofocus motor to set the distance of the lens from the film. The shutter is released by fully depressing the release button. After the exposure has been made, the film is automatically advanced to the next frame.

The frame counter window is situated behind the release button. This counts not only forwards, but also backwards when the film is rewound into its cassette. To the left of the counter is the film rewind button and, below that, the release catch for film rewind, called film rewind lever in the instruction book. The film can only be rewound by sliding the release catch to the right and then depressing the rewind button.

To the right of the viewfinder prism is the aperture dial at the back and the shutter speed dial at the front. The shutter speed dial also serves as the main switch. Apart from the shutter speed values it has an "L" (lock) setting. At the **L** setting the camera is switched off and the release cannot be triggered. The shooting mode in which you wish to operate the camera is selected by a combination of shutter speed on the shutter speed dial and aperture on the aperture dial. The following combinations are possible:

○ If the shutter speed dial is set to **A** and the aperture dial to **S**, the camera will function in program mode. This means that the aperture and the shutter speed are automatically set by the camera.

○ If the shutter speed dial is set to **A** and the aperture dial to an aperture value, the camera will function in aperture priority mode. This means the camera will automatically select a suitable shutter speed for the selected aperture.

○ If the aperture value is set to **S** and a shutter speed is selected on the shutter speed dial, the camera will function in shutter speed priority mode. This means it will automatically select a suitable aperture for the selected shutter speed.

○ If a value is selected on the aperture dial and also a shutter speed on the shutter speed dial, the camera will function in manual mode and the automatic exposure mode is de-activated.

On top of the viewfinder prism is the accessory shoe with the flash contacts. By using a Nikon system flashgun it is possible to shoot in TTL flash mode. If you have the special Nikon AF flash SB-20, or the SB-22, it is even possible to obtain automatic focusing in total darkness. This is the reason for the extra contact in the accessory shoe.

The red LED, on the right next to the front edge of the shutter speed dial indicates correct film loading and film transport. If the LED is continuously lit, then it is indicating either "film transport blocked", or "end of film". If the LED flashes continuously, it is indicating that the self-timer is counting down.

To the left of the viewfinder prism is the self-timer button. Slight pressure on this button will automatically release the shutter after about 10 seconds. To cancel the self-timer press it gently a second time.

On the rear edge of the camera, between the prism housing and the self-timer butten, is a symbol consisting of a line through a circle. This indicates the film plane and is particularly useful in close-up work.

Operating elements of the F-401

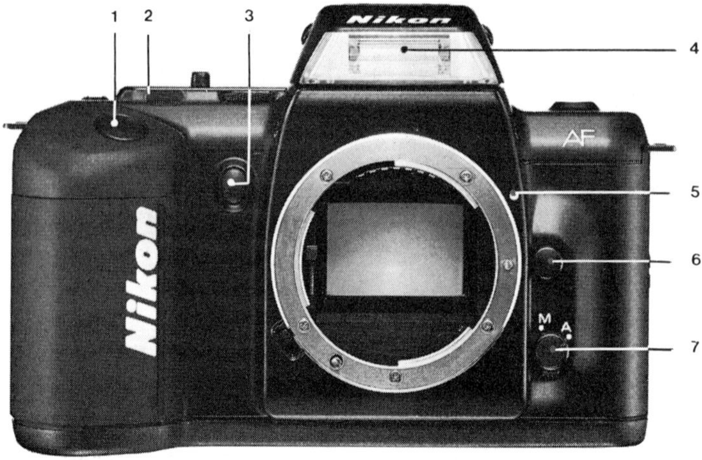

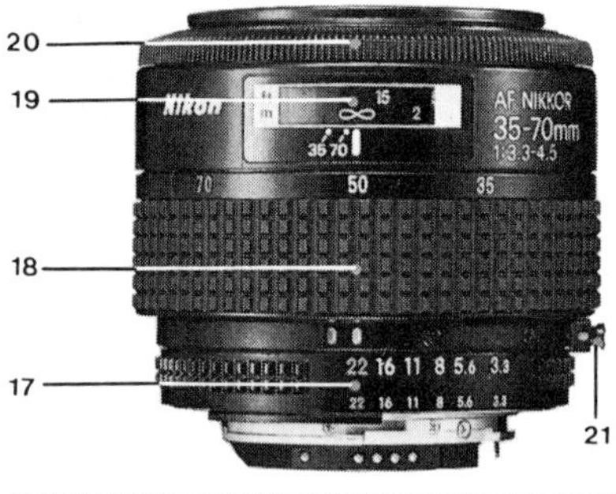

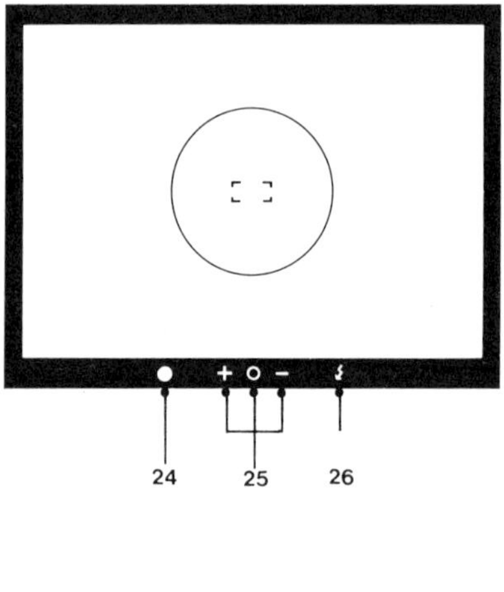

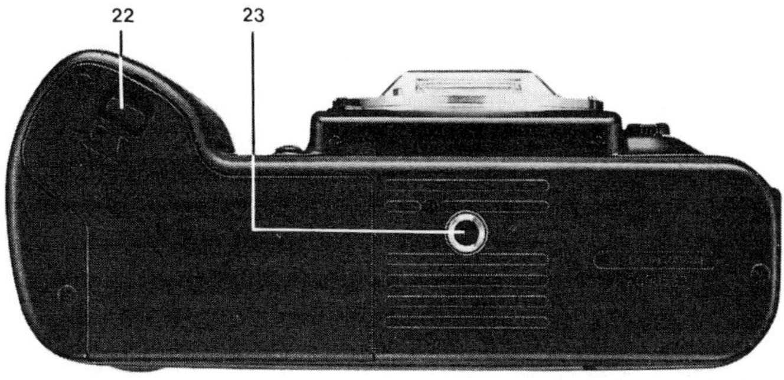

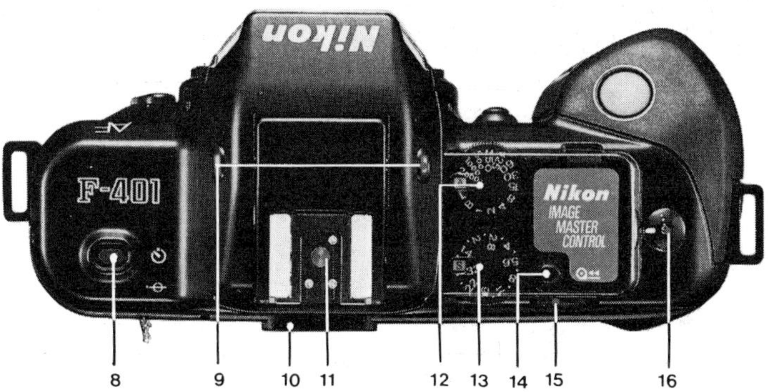

1 release
2 self-timer display
3 AEL button (Auto Exposure Lock)
4 integrated TTL flash
5 lens mounting index
6 lens release button
7 focus mode selector
8 self-timer button
9 flash lock release buttons
10 viewfinder eyepiece
11 accessory shoe
12 shutter speed dial
13 aperture dial
14 film rewind button
15 film rewind lever
16 frame counter
17 aperture index
18 zoom ring
19 distance scale window
20 focusing ring for manual focusing
21 minimum aperture lock
22 battery compartment lock release
23 tripod screw thread
24 focus indicator LED
25 exposure indicator LEDs
26 flash-ready light

Now let's examine the standard zoom Nikon AF 35-70mm, f/3.3-f/4.5 from the top. At the very front of the lens is the manual distance-setting ring, which is needed with even an autofocus lens in some critical focusing situations. Behind that is the distance scale window. The bold white marker has several functions, just as with most Nikon lenses. It serves not only as the marker for both the distance scale and aperture scale, but also as the marker for aligning the lens and camera when changing lenses. Behind this is the ring for selecting the focal length. Further back is the aperture scale and the aperture read-out scale: this second aperture scale is not used with the F-401, but is for use when the lens is mounted on other Nikon cameras where it is used to convey the set aperture value to the viewfinder. An important facility with Nikon lenses is the ability to lock the aperture. This is necessary in the program modes when the aperture has to be locked at the largest numerical value, i.e. the smallest possible aperture setting. The minimum aperture lock button is situated on the right-hand side on the lens. At the very rear, close to the bayonet, is the black control ring to transfer the aperture values from lens to camera. The camera's computer will recognize by the operation of this aperture switch and by the control curve of the lens, that the lens is, in fact, set to the largest aperture value.

Looking at the camera from the front, on the top left-hand side just above the shutter release is the red LED mentioned above. Underneath that, between the handgrip and the lens, is the auto exposure lock button (AEL). As long as this button is kept depressed, the triple sensor metering is de-activated in all automatic modes and the last exposure value metered in centre-weighted metering is stored, to be recalled when the shutter release button is depressed, regardless of any changes in lighting and subject conditions that may have taken place in the meantime. To the left, beneath the bayonet bezel, minimum aperture lock.

Above the bayonet is the small, but quite powerful, integrated TTL flash. To bring this into action, depress the two release buttons on either side of the flash housing.

With the lens removed you can see the seven contacts for the new AF lenses, located at the top, inside the camera bayonet. These contacts are used to transfer lens data such as lens speed, focal length, and setting distance for focusing. These values are then used by the AF computer to calculate the necessary focusing values. At the bottom left of the bayonet is a pivoted metal pin; this is the motor coupling for automatic lens focusing. To the right of the bayonet is the black lens release button.

Beneath the lens release button is the focus mode selector:

- **M** is the setting for manual focusing with electronic focus assist indication, provided the attached lens is fast enough;
- **A** is the setting for automatic focusing.

Looking at the camera from the back, and with the back panel open, we see on the left the film rewind fork protruding into the film cassette chamber. To the right of it are six contacts for DX coding. These are used to read the film speed from the cassette. The shutter blinds in the middle must never be touched when removing or inserting a film as they are very delicate and touching them could cause irreparable damage.

The viewfinder eyepiece can accept correction lenses, an eye cup, or an eyepiece cover that should be attached to prevent entry of light during long exposures when the photographer's eye is removed from the viewfinder.

To the right-hand side of the camera interior is the automatic film threading device. This consists of the film take-up spool, the film guide track and the film sprocket roller. The red marker is the film leader index and indicates how far the film has to be pulled out of the cassette to be properly loaded. The film pressure plate on the back panel also must not be touched, as the film will not lie completely flat if the pressure plate is distorted. On closing the back panel you can see through the film window if a film is loaded. A special feature that was introduced with the F-301 and

F-501, and included in the F-401, is the film advance indicator. This rotates to show that the film is loading and advancing correctly.

Looking at the camera from below, there is very little of note. Beneath the handgrip is the catch that unlocks the battery compartment and in the centre is the tripod socket.

Now let's look through the viewfinder. In the middle we see the corner outlines of the rectangular metering field, which is the autofocus target area. The surrounding 12mm diameter circle indicates the area of centre-weighted light metering. The matt field of the focusing screen is specially useful when manual focusing is necessary. Below the matt field is the display panel, with one red LED for checking for correct exposure. Illumination of this LED means that the setting is satisfactory. Then there are the red plus and minus signs to indicate risk of under- or over-exposure. On the far right is the red flash symbol for flash control, and to the far left is the green focusing indicator.

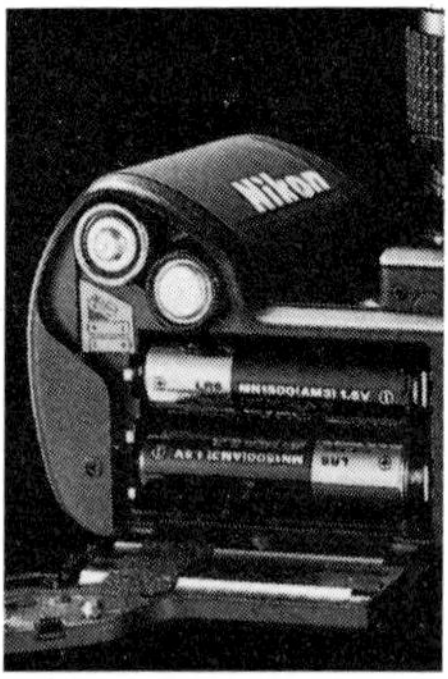

Four AA-size batteries fit the battery compartment of the F-401. Alkaline batteries, and also rechargeable batteries, are recommended.

No More Worries About Batteries

I am sure it will not come as a surprise to learn that a camera such as the F-401, having motorized film transport and another motor for focusing the lens, needs batteries. The only question is, how well has Nikon solved the problem of energy supply? Very well, it seems. Four AA cells power not only the two motors of the F-401, but also the camera's electronics for metering, setting and operation of shutter and mirror. The supply voltage of 6V (4 x 1.5V) is ample. This is on the assumption that as long as there is enough energy for the motors, there must be enough to measure the lighting conditions. If the voltage is lower than 1.3V per cell, then there is a possibility that the camera will no longer release the shutter. If it does activate the shutter, then it is still quite safe, even with exhausted batteries, because the exposure reading and triggering of the shutter itself requires scarcely any energy at all; the main drain on the energy supply occurs when the exposure has been made and the motor is activated to move the film to the next frame. If the batteries run down and drop below the minimum voltage requirement because of the heavy load imposed by the motor drive, it is still no great tragedy. They will recover and you can take another picture. In emergencies it is possible to make quite a few exposures, even with nearly run-down batteries, without risk of incorrect exposure. You will have to wait, though, between frames until the voltage level recovers sufficiently. (This is no tip for Scrooges – I DO mean in an emergency!)

Nikon specify the use of alkaline batteries in the AA size, which are available almost everywhere. Under ideal conditions a fresh set will last for 50, 36-exposure films. If you are using flash much of the time, then the batteries are likely to last for no more than 10 – 20 films. Rechargeable nickel-cadmium batteries of the same size are also quite suitable. However, these tend to discharge spontaneously when not in use and should therefore to be used with some reservations. I would recommend that these are never left in the camera but are kept in a suitable recharger when not in use. The ordinary zinc-carbon batteries may be used as a real emergency solution. This type of battery does not retain a steady voltage level and performs poorly at low temperatures. They should only be used therefore in extreme emergencies.

If you have already been using electronic cameras you will know that the battery's greatest enemy is the cold. This applies to most batteries used in cameras, which are often small button cells. The F-401 is a praiseworthy exception – equipped with four fresh AA-size or a set of freshly recharged batteries it will work in temperatures down to –10° C. I would not advise such experiments, but it should work directly from the freezer! But at these low temperatures you cannot expect the same output as in normal temperatures.

The following rules for the handling of batteries in the F-401 should be observed:

- Alkaline batteries, size AA, are most suitable.
- Freshly charged nickel cadmium batteries of the same size are also suitable.
- Zinc-carbon batteries should be used only in an emergency.
- Always keep a set of spare batteries in reserve. Always buy only fresh batteries. Check the date on them or ask your dealer to check the voltage.
- Replace the batteries at least once a year with a completely new set. Even if the camera has not been used, batteries slowly discharge with age.
- In winter keep batteries in a warm place (15 to 20°C).

Another piece of good advice: the automatic cut-off controlling the viewfinder LEDs also serves as a battery level indicator. If the LEDs are extinguished after about 8 sec. then the batteries are good; if after 2 sec. then you should change the set.

Film Loading is Child's Play

Loading the film should present no problems, even from the start. Slide down the camera-back lock release to open the camera back and insert the film cassette in the chamber. Hold the film cassette down with your left thumb and pull the

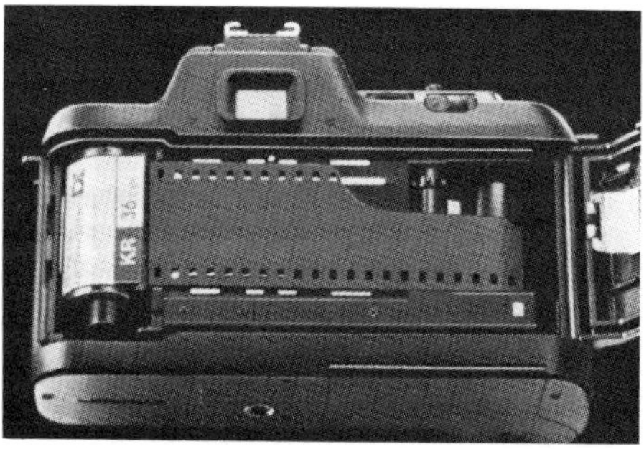

Film loading is fast and easy with automatic film loading and film transport.

film end with your right hand until it reaches the red marker. Check that the sprockets are engaged with the transport perforations of the film, then close the camera back and fully depress the shutter release. The film will then be automatically advanced to frame 1. The only problem that you could possibly encounter is if the film has been pulled too far, or not far enough. I have loaded a considerable number of films into the F-401 and found that one millimetre more or less makes no difference. Whether or not you have loaded the film properly is immediately obvious. One glance at the film transport indicator on the back plate is sufficient.

Rewinding the film is also very easy. The film advance stops automatically at the end of the roll and the self-timer indicator LED lights up for a few seconds. While sliding the film rewind lever to the right, simultaneously push the film rewind button, both of which are situated on the top right-hand side of the camera. The F-401 rewinds the film completely into the cassette. This has the advantage that you will never mistake a fresh film for an exposed one. Another advantage, a completely rewound film does not allow the operator in the processing lab to pull the film out too fast, a process which could cause scratches and dust-attracting electrostatic charges, or even sparks.

If it is a high-speed film, about ISO 1000 or faster, and if it is returned completely into the cassette, light could enter through the narrow slit and the first few frames may be fogged as a result. As a precaution, cover the slit with some black adhesive tape and place the film immediately in a light-tight container, or wrap it in some aluminium foil to keep it safe.

Automatic Film Transport

I admit, I have never been a fan of winders and motor drives. These "film destruction devices" are in most cases too loud in operation for taking candid shots. The motor of the F-401 is by no means the loudest, but its humming is definitely audible. However, as we have opted for autofocus, we are already putting up with the noise from the AF motor, so the additional sound of the film transport must also be accepted. In any case this little difficulty can be overcome by taking into account beforehand that a snapshot has to be right first time if you want your subject to be unaware of your activity. On the other hand, the integrated motor has its advantages. Just consider automatic film loading, which does work perfectly with the F-401. The automatic rewind is another obvious advantage.

The motorized film transport is also invaluable for copying and close-ups. Even if the camera is mounted on a tripod, manual winding always disturbs its alignment. In this situation it is best to use the self-timer, to avoid camera shake (first focus, then depress self-timer).

Then there are the pleasures of series shots of moving subjects. I found the motor drive invaluable when trying to catch a wedding party spilling out from the church, action on the football pitch, or children at play – in all these situations the camera can be kept against the eye with no need to find the subject again after film transport. The subject stays in the viewfinder and the number of successful shots is increased.

Advantages and Disadvantages of DX Coding

The F-401 has, like most other modern cameras, the facility

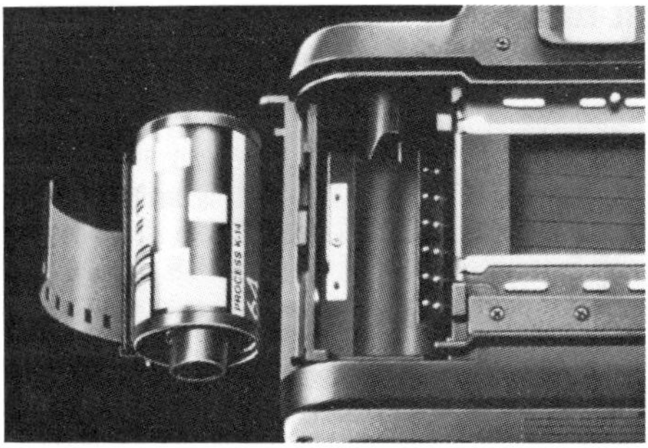

The six electrical contacts in the film chamber are used to convey information to the camera computer, which interprets the resistance pattern of DX-coded cassettes and automatically sets the film speed.

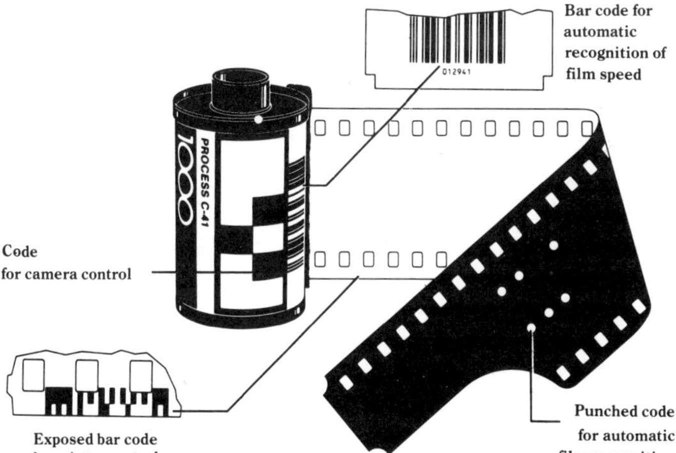

to read the film speed automatically. Most cassettes of film now include a coded, machine-readable information strip for this purpose. The code includes the visible bar codes (black lines) indicating manufacturer, type of film and film speed, which are primarily intended for processing purposes at the lab. Similar bar codes can be found on the edges of many films and some have punched codes at the beginning of the film, or on the film leader. Then there is the resistance code, which is conveyed by polished metallic (low resistance) and painted (high resistance) areas which are interpreted by the camera and directly transferred via electrical contacts into the

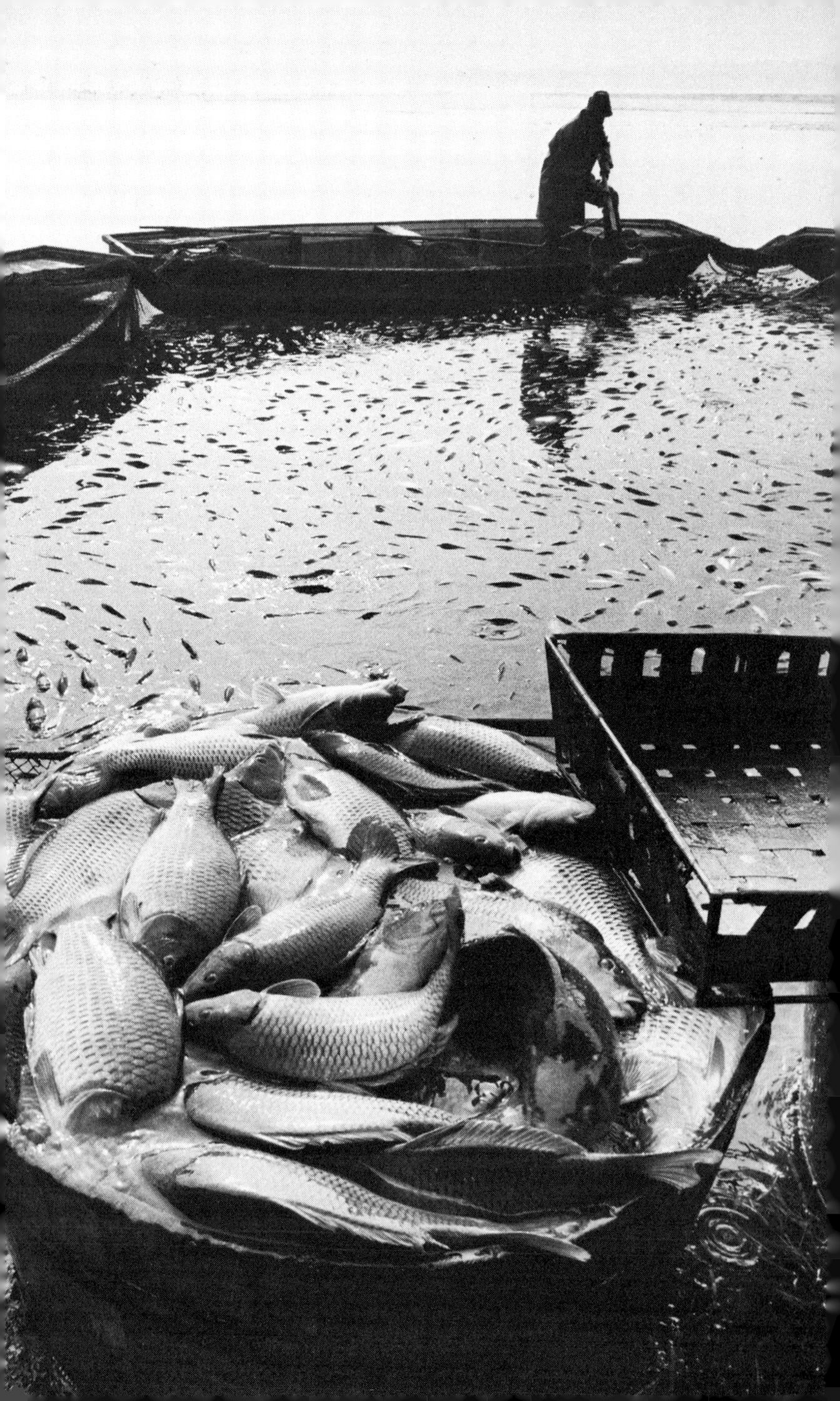

exposure microcomputer.

Problems will arise, however, if you load a film that has no DX coding. The F-401 will assume that this film has a speed of ISO 100 and expose it accordingly. If you are using an ISO 200, or a 400 colour print film, then the resulting negatives should not be too bad. However, if you are shooting with colour slide film you will end up with inferior quality transparencies. Another problem in reading the DX codes could arise if you are using a film straight from the refrigerator. The condensation could influence the DX coding and lead to incorrect readings. The same problems can arise if your fingers are sweaty or dirty. The resistance readings could be wrong and lead to incorrect speed settings.

The following rules in handling film should therefore be observed:

- Always use only DX coded film. This should present no problems as this is now sold world-wide.
- Make sure always that the cassette is clean and dry when you are inserting it in the camera.

The entire scene was captured by the use of a wide-angle lens. The emphasised foreground with the basket of fish creates a strong base. For full effect the foreground had to be very sharp against an acceptably sharp background. Aperture priority is obviously the best exposure mode to use in this situation where you can choose a suitable aperture to control the depth of field. Photo: Rudolf Dietrich

A Good Camera Deserves a Good Film

Considering how much you have just spent on a new camera and excellent lens, you should not haggle about the price of a roll of film. But is the more expensive film really better? If we concentrate our argument on colour print film, then we have to say ''no''. The products from the large manufacturers such as Fuji, Kodak, Agfa and Konica are of comparable quality, and Scotch too is very much in the same quality bracket. If the main purpose of your photography is holiday or family snaps, then I would say you could buy whichever is being offered at the best price. If we consider slide films then some essential differences are noticeable. You will have to ask yourself the following questions: should I buy Kodachrome 25 or 64, which are considerably more expensive than any other, but produce excellent sharpness, or am I more interested in the full poster colours of Fujichrome RD 100 which costs considerably less? Price is not the only criterion, different films can have different qualities which will meet different needs.

Some Good Tips on Films

When buying and storing film there are a few rules worth remembering:

- ○ Always buy fresh film from a specialist dealer. Out-of-date films in the special offer tray are usually not worth having.
- ○ If your main interest lies in colour prints, then I would say an ISO 200 film, such as Fuijicolor Super HR 200 or Kodacolor Gold 200, would be suitable for most purposes.
- ○ For colour slide photography it is advisable to keep two different film speeds in reserve. To obtain good quality I

would suggest one at ISO 50, 64 or 100, and then an ISO 400 or 1000 for situations when the light fails or you are dealing with fast-moving subjects.

- Always keep your spare films in the fridge, or even the freezer. Before using one leave it for one to two hours to warm up, otherwise you could have condensation problems.
- An exposed film should be processed as soon as possible. If this is impossible, then store it in a cool place.

Criteria for Choosing the Right Film

How do we distinguish a good film from a bad one? The answer is relatively simple: a good film is finely-grained, covers a wide range of exposure values, and reproduces the subject with great sharpness and natural colour rendition.

That the fine grain of the film is an important criterion is a well-known fact. Just try and project a grainy colour slide onto a 2m high screen or enlarge a colour negative for a 30x35cm print. It is unpleasant to see the sky, which we are used to seeing as a uniform blue area, broken down into coloured grains. The graininess of a film is generally dependent on its speed; the slower the film, the finer the grain. An ISO 100 film of one manufacturer will therefore always be more finely-grained than an ISO 200 from the same manufacturer.

Then there is the sharpness, i.e. how many fine details are recognizable in the picture. The sharpness is determined by two factors: the resolution and the contour sharpness. The resolution is a measure of how many fine parallel lines may be distinguished per millimeter. The contour sharpness defines how sharply the bright/dark edges of the subject are reproduced in the picture. Both of these factors depend, amongst others, on the graininess of the film, and these, in turn, reinforce each other to a certain degree. Namely: the finer grained a film, the greater its resolution, and the better its contour sharpness. This explains why it is impossible to find an exceedingly fast film that also has good contour sharpness. As a rule, the ISO 100 film will always produce better sharpness than the ISO 200 of the same make. If we now compare films of the same speed but from different manufacturers we find that while some will tend to be better in respect of graininess, others excel in their sharpness. So, for example, Fujicolor Super HR 200 is finer-grained than Kodacolor Gold 200, but Kodacolor is better as regards sharpness. If we disregard colour rendition and concentrate only on sharpness and grain, then the finer-grained film will be better suited for portraits, a case where a large grain is particularly unpleasant. If you are concentrating on a series of shots of landscapes, on the other hand, then Kodacolor will produce better results by showing finer details.

Exposure range is another important criterion in the consideration of film quality. Until recently it used to be considered the norm to accept a subject contrast of 1:300 (i.e details could still be discerned in the light and the dark areas where the lightest tones are three hundred times brighter than the darkest ones). Improvements in photographic emulsions presented us with a new generation of films with exposure ranges of up to 1:1000 and more. This wide range is beneficial in other respects. The greater the exposure range of a film, the greater the exposure latitude. Subjects with medium contrast may in this way be overexposed by up to two stops or underexposed by up to one stop on Fuji Super HR 200 or Kodacolor Gold 200 without affecting the final picture quality. Even three stops underexposure and four stops overexposure should result in some quite acceptable pictures. In cases where the available light is not quite sufficient you may expose such a 200 ISO film quite easily as ISO 400 or even ISO 800, without fear of producing a bad picture (with the F-401 this will only be possible in manual operation). Therefore I suggest using these films as general purpose films for most situations. The same does not hold true for colour slide films. These have a much smaller exposure range and will show noticeable deterioration in quality by under- or overexposure from as little as $^1/_3$ to $^2/_3$ stops, always depending on the type of film.

In the matter of colour rendition, opinions can differ. This is definitely a question of personal taste and not an objective criterion. One thing is obvious: the colours should be correctly reproduced: carmine red should be carmine red, and orange-red should be orange-red. But if all the red nuances are reduced to a uniform red ketchup, then this is a sure sign that the quality of the film is not what it is supposed to be. Not only the hue but also its saturation should be correctly reproduced. However, modern colour technology is quite capable of producing satisfactory saturation and some are apt to exaggerate it. Luckily, the colours do not bear down on us like a Smartie advert, as used to be the trend in the 70's, but some over-emphasis is still a question of taste of whether it is an advantage to see the reproduced image in more glowing colours than the original. The glowing colours of a landscape will immediately indicate to the viewer "beautiful weather". A slight over-emphasis of brighter colours may also be an advantage in "poor-weather shots", which counteract an overall impression of grey dreariness. Moreover, some films that tend towards greater colour intensity often reproduce details in the shady sections in a warmer colour. Colour-neutral films, on the other hand, may tend to show these as slightly bluish. If it is important to achieve the greatest possible correctness of colour rendition, then Agfachrome 50 RS or 100 RS would be suitable for slide photography, but for general photography I would recommend the slightly more colour intensive Ektachrome 100 or Fujichrome RD 100 for colour slides.

Colour Slides or Prints?

The projected image of a good slide has colour and tonal reproduction that is unrivalled by any other form of photographic reproduction. The glowing colours and the fine details in light and shade are reproduced in unsurpassed brilliance and vividness. The reason for this is that slide film is higher in contrast than a colour print. But the delights that a colour slide can bring require some degree of expertise to achieve.

Because slide films are so high in contrast they are also very sensitive to incorrect exposure. Half a stop under- or overexposure can have adverse effects, especially with high-contrast subjects. Also, if you think you could produce perfect prints from your slides, you will be disappointed. Admittedly, it is quite cheap these days to get prints made, and their quality is usually quite acceptable. The problem starts when you want to make enlargements from your slides, as colours, which are specially brilliant and clear in their projected image, are often reproduced imperfectly. Only images with small brightness ranges and saturated colours are produced equally well or even better as prints than they were on slides.

The strength of colour negative film lies in the colour prints it can produce. This is true even if the quality of the prints from the large processing laboratories is not always the best. But this problem also exists for slide film, as these too are not always perfectly processed. However, it can be said, that, in general, slide films are usually better processed than colour prints. The reason for this is that the colour print has to undergo three stages: film development, enlargement and printing. This means that there are two more steps where the quality can vary. But provided the film was correctly exposed and it was properly processed by the laboratory, you should obtain good enlargements from both types of images.

The answer to the question of whether to use slide or print film must therefore be that if you consider prints your medium, then you will have to choose print film, but if you value the quality of the projected image, then you will want to use a slide film. If you like both, then you have to use them alternately – or perhaps use a second camera body to be able to use both types of film at the same time.

Select the Right Film for the Job

It is true that the quality with respect to sharpness and graininess of the modern ISO 1000 and 1600 films offered by many manufacturers is surprisingly good. But technological progress increases our expectations and the quality of lower speed films has improved in line with that of the high speed films. The latest improvements have brought a range of low and medium speed films of excellent quality such as Kodacolor Gold, Fujicolor Super HR, Agfa XRi and Konica SR-V. Scotch, too, have also improved their HR films. To obtain maximum sharpness and colour saturation use the ISO 50, 64 and 100 films. If you want to be prepared for all, or most, eventualities, then ISO 200 is a good bet. If you are taking pictures under low lighting conditions, or if your subject is moving fast, perhaps in sport or play, then you would be well-advised to use an ISO 400 or even 1600 film. Even if you are holidaying in the sunny south it is always a good idea to have a few fast films handy.

Which film for what photographic situation is a different question. It seems quite obvious that if you photograph in low lighting conditions the best films to use are the ISO 1000 and ISO 1600 films. However, be careful not to overestimate the ability of these speeds. In a normally-lit living room, using an ISO 1000 film, you cannot give any less exposure than $^1/_{60}$ sec. at f/2.8 and the lighting conditions in a normally-lit gymnasium would not be much better. Even very bright floodlighting will give only a few extra stops.

Another aspect that is often not sufficiently appreciated is the irregular, poorly-lit area of a general subject. It is possible in individual cases to produce a lovely romantic image of a subject lit by candlelight, but usually these efforts are quite worthless, even with an ISO 1600 film. You will usually see a great deal of the candle, but not much else. Fast films replace flash only in certain situations. Of course, it is not always possible to use flash, but even then I would think twice before using an ISO 1000 or 1600 film, even if camera-shake is a real

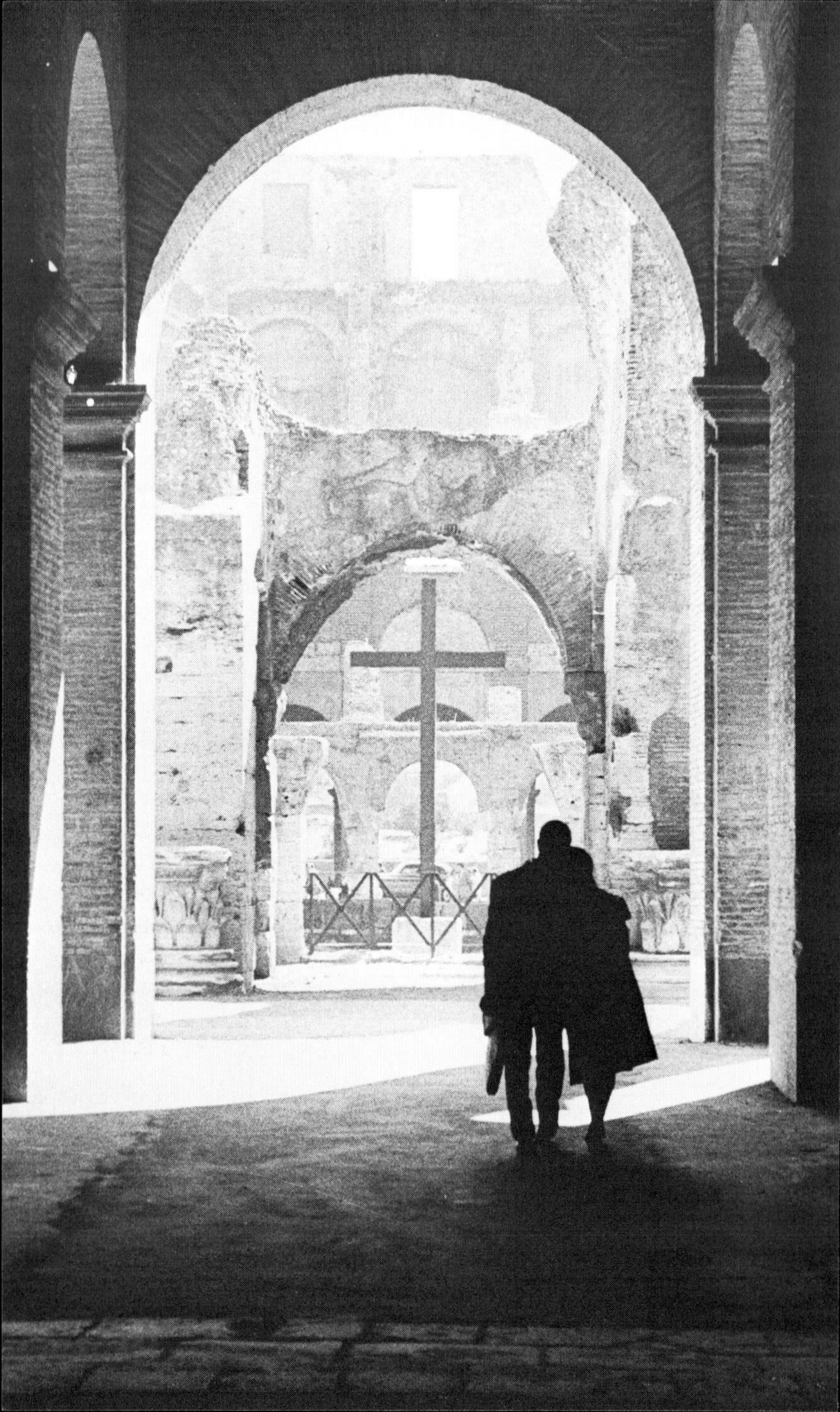

problem. Although some of these films are surprisingly fine-grained, they are all slightly inferior as regards colour reproduction. The question therefore is whether a gain in film speed equivalent to one or two stops compensates for the advantages of the finer-grained and well-tried ISO 400 film? One should never choose the film according to the premise: "as fast as possible, to allow for exposure reserves". Better: "always choose the film speed just fast enough to stay within the limits of camera-shake if the lighting conditions are poor".

Black-and-White Photography Is Not Dead!

As a photographer you will almost certainly use colour film right from the start. This is quite justifiable and understandable. Modern colour photography presents comparatively few problems and is relatively cheap compared with the traditional black-and-white process. Badly-developed colour slides are a rarity and if you use colour print film you usually get at least reasonable quality from the processing lab. Today, black-and-white prints of equal, or even better, quality are almost out of the amateur's price range.

Black-and-white photography is an art in itself. The colours and contrasts of the subject have to be translated into tones of grey. Nevertheless a good black-and-white picture lacks nothing; in fact some subjects are even better in this form than would be possible in colour. But if you wish to express yourself in this medium you will almost certainly have to set up a darkroom and do your own processing and printing. It

Subjects with high contrast are not ideal for colour photography. A black-and-white composition is often particularly effective. This photograph was exposed for the shadow areas. Care in film development and printing and careful choice of paper grade are the secret of this view. Photo: Rudolf Dietrich starts with development of your own film, which has to suit the type of film used, then you have to use the correct type and grade of paper to produce a good enlargement. Then there is a whole range of little tricks such as shading, masking, and so on. But this necessity to print your own pictures need not be a disadvantage; on the contrary, it can be a great source of enjoyment and satisfaction.

If you want to try black-and-white photography for yourself, then I would recommend you use Ilford XP-1 film. This is a monochrome film using colour technology. It handles high contrast subjects and has large exposure latitude. You can have it developed by one of the same large photographic labs where you send your colour films.

This was easily captured with the F-401 in program mode. The focal length of the zoom was set to 100mm and the triple sensor metering adjusted the exposure perfectly for this rather difficult subject. Photo: Wolf Huber

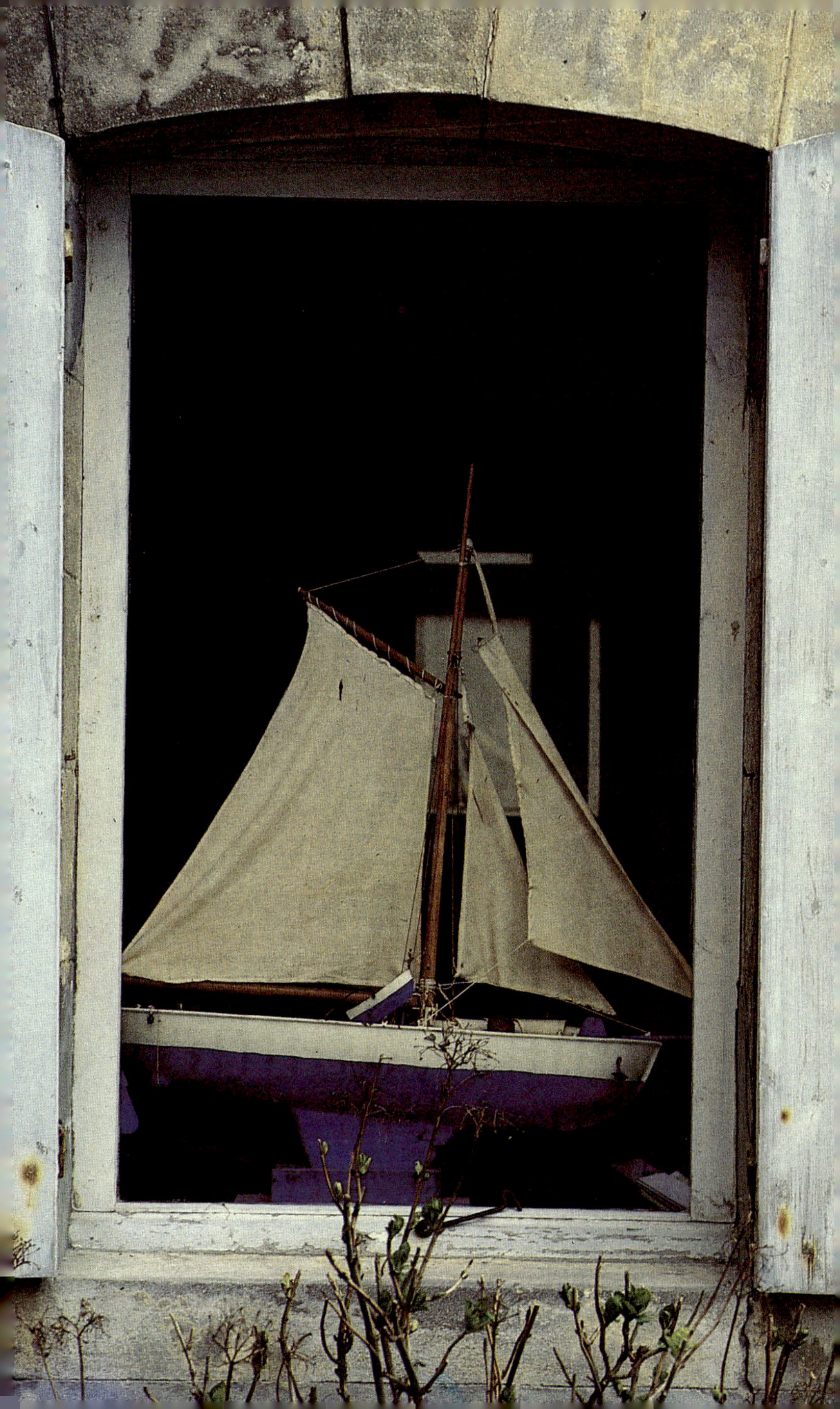

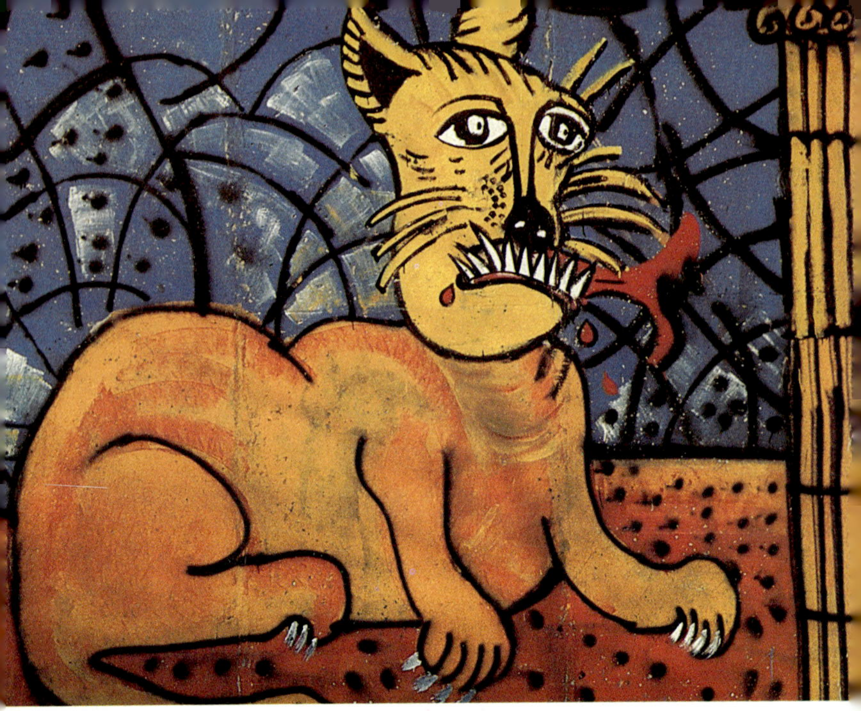

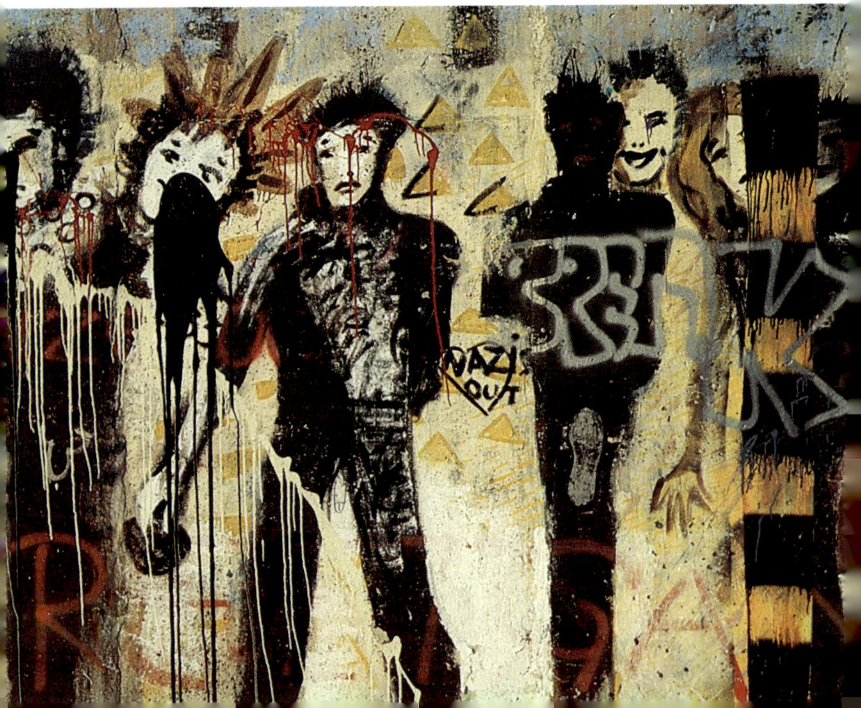
NAZI OUT

Make Your Own Film Test!

As you have seen, there are certain criteria to be observed in the choice of film, but these do not depend only on the shooting situation, but also on your own personal taste. The colour reproduction qualities of certain films could be the subject of almost unlimited discussion. The final word as to which is the best – the most suitable film for your own needs and preferences, will be your own decision. The various manufacturers now present the amateur photographer with such a wide range of high-quality films, each excellent, that the choice is entirely up to you!

Graffiti can be an interesting subject. These two were taken at the Berlin wall at a distance of about 8m with a 90mm lens. Shorter distances and a shorter focal length could have caused converging verticals.

Photos: Michael Huber

Automatically Better Pictures with Image Master Control

The description "Image Master Control" refers to the integrated central microcomputer. This computer calculates and controls all the camera functions: film transport, film speed setting, autofocus, exposure metering, exposure control, exposure correction and flash control. All these functions make photography with the F-401 just as easy as using a fully-automatic pocket camera. Incorrect camera handling is almost impossible, technically bad pictures, i.e. out-of-focus or incorrectly exposed pictures, are now very much a thing of the past.

Fully Automatic Picture Taking

Fully automatic control by the Image Master Control System starts with film loading. The film is loaded automatically and the film speed read into the exposure system by DX coding.

Focusing is similarly "automatic". In the **A** focusing mode the shutter will only be released if the autofocus has set the distance correctly. The Image Master Control will block the release as long as focusing has not been effected, or is impossible to set. However, the camera computer cannot know which subject detail is the one you wish to focus on. Is it Grandma right in front or is it Auntie at the back who should be featured? You will have to decide the important section in

Top: in situations where technically perfect shots are not possible the release will be blocked.

Centre: in situations where technically perfect shots are not possible, the camera computer will issue a warning and suggest a remedy.

Bottom: in many situations the photographer has to make decisions and perform actions which require a certain amount of skill and experience. The camera computer of the F-401 is able to perform many of these automatically.

RELEASE IS BLOCKED:

- Danger of over- or underexposure:
- Lens not focused properly
- Film end
- Flash not ready
- Lens aperture ring not engaged

CAMERA ISSUES WARNINGS:

- Danger of over- or underexposure:
- AF focusing not possible
- Danger of camera shake
- Film speed too high for TTL flash control
- Film end
- Lens aperture ring not engaged
- Flash recommended
- Flash not ready
- Fill-in flash necessary

AUTOMATIC:

- Exposure corrections in difficult shooting situations
- Additional use of fill-in flash
- Change over to high-speed program when using longer focal length lenses
- Fill-in flash balances brightness of foreground and background

your picture, but totally unsharp pictures will be a thing of the past.

Serious errors in exposure will also be almost impossible with the F-401. The camera computer assesses by a three-section metering method not only the subject brightness, but also the distribution of light and dark areas. The Image Master Control automatically recognizes from this three-field metering if any exposure corrections are necessary. Backlit shots, unusually bright subjects, available light shots, etc., are recognized with a great degree of certainty. Any exposure corrections or the additional use of flash is automatically performed.

The Image Master Control also counteracts the danger of camera-shake as far as possible, and without dominating the photographer's actions. In the fully-automatic program mode it will automatically switch to the fast shutter speed program when a long-focus lens is used. In all automatic exposure modes the camera computer will signal danger of camera-shake by the flashing red exposure indicator LED in the viewfinder if the calculated shutter speed is longer than $^1/_{30}$ sec.

Special attention is paid to flash control. Whenever the lighting conditions are sufficiently poor that flash may be needed it is automatically indicated to the photographer who can then switch on the flash if he wants to use it. The amount of flash is then assessed by TTL metering and automatically controlled. Another special bonus is the automatic selection of a suitable aperture when using TTL flash in program, or shutter speed priority modes. Depending on available light and subject contrast (fill-in flash) the Image Master Control will select a suitable aperture, so that the brightnesses of the background and the foreground are adjusted. This is a job that in manual operation takes time and is usually too difficult for the average photographer to assess.

To summarise, one can say that the Image Master Control not only prevents mistakes, it ensures perfect exposure in many photographic situations. It does this by effecting automatic exposure corrections, which even an experienced photographer would have been able to do only after taking measurements and working out the necessary manual corrections, all of which takes time and is performed much quicker by the F-401.

Manual Operation with the Aid of Image Master Control

There are a number of shooting situations, and subjects, which are not suited to automatic exposure in program mode. For example, sports photography is usually better undertaken in shutter speed priority mode, whilst landscapes, architecture and portraits, where depth of field is important, will be better taken in aperture priority mode. Then there are situations where the triple-sensor light metering does not supply reliable answers. In this case you can switch to centre-weighted metering with auto exposure lock (AEL).

The shutter speed priority and aperture priority modes together with auto exposure lock allow precise control by the photographer and may be considered superior to the Image Master Control in these situations. These facilities are thus described by Nikon as the override functions for free, creative use of the F-401. However, any initial and subsequent functions performed by the photographer, are still controlled by the Image Master Control. If the calculated exposure results in danger of over- or underexposure, or focusing has not been effected, then the appropriate warning signals are given.

Adventurous photographers can make use of the facility to completely de-activate the Image Master Control. In shooting mode **M** the lens may be manually focused. In some situations, or with subjects that are not suited to autofocus, this could be an advantage. But it is now possible to release the shutter even if the subject is not correctly focused. The situation is similar for manual selection of exposure. Although the photographer is assisted by the electronic display of exposure in the viewfinder, the camera will not protest even if you are setting completely random numbers on the shutter speed and aperture dials and if you ignore the warnings you may end up with totally over- or underexposed pictures.

The manual exposure modes of the F-401 are of little importance in the majority of shooting situations. It is generally better to rely on the sophisticated facilities of the Image Master Control. Only in situations when you are sure that your manual settings will be more appropriate than the automatic control should you disregard the electronic guidance.

In some situations the experienced photographer's own judgement will be better than that of the camera computer. After all it only knows what the Nikon engineers have programmed it to do. There are, of course, limits of this preprogrammed "knowledge" and its ability to assess the readings. After all, the camera computer cannot know which part of the subject is of particular interest, and what importance is assigned to the remaining parts, or whether the photographer wishes to represent the backlit subjects as silhouettes against the bright sky or should the flash be used to lighten the foreground?

As you can see, despite all technical progress the photographer is still the important factor in taking good pictures.

"Mother and child" must be one of the most popular subjects, but the figures are not always placed suitably in the frame. We have all seen pictures where the kitchen is more easily recognized than the main subjects. It is also no improvement if the flash is allowed to release its full power into the baby's eyes. Use a medium telephoto lens for intimate shots such as this. If a flash is necessary, put a diffuser in front of the reflector. Don't worry if it takes a whole roll of film, it should give you at least some good frames. Photo: Rudolf Dietrich

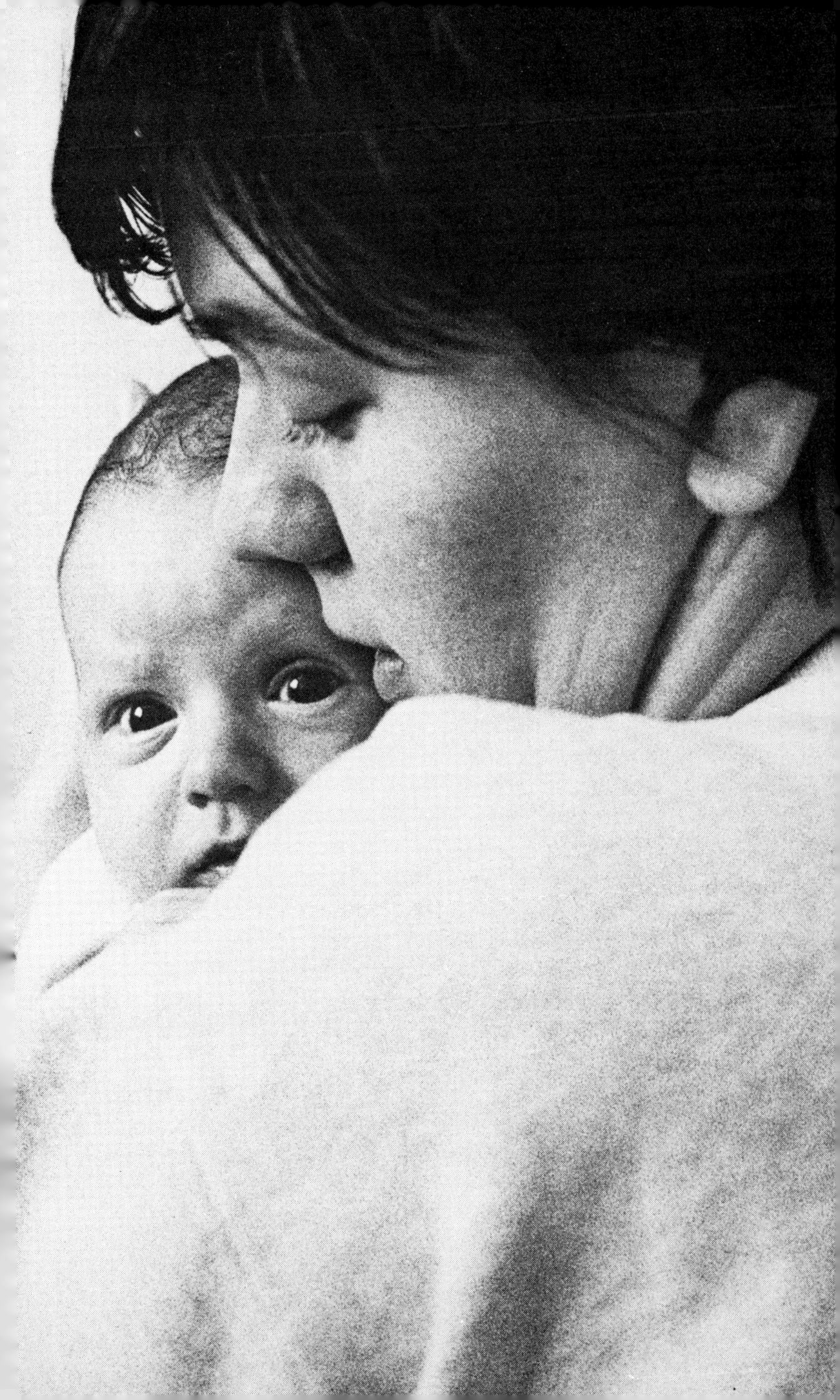

The Autofocus

Compared with the automatic focusing of the F-501, the autofocus of the F-401 has been further improved. The light sensitivity in particular has been increased. I can vouch for this after several weeks testing when I put about twenty films through the camera. Obviously, there are still some situations where the autofocus of the F-401 is unsuitable, but in all general applications it works perfectly. In situations where the autofocus ran into trouble, manual focusing was also very difficult. Thanks to autofocus, focusing has never been so simple and so fast.

This is How Autofocus is Used

Setting the shooting mode selector to **A** makes unsharp pictures a thing of the past. In this shooting mode the automatic focusing has priority: the release button will remain locked as long as the autofocus has not focused correctly. In practice this means you point the camera at the subject, keeping the main subject within the rectangular focusing field at the centre of the viewfinder, depress the release down to the first pressure level (i.e. not fully) and wait until the green in-focus indicator lights up to show that the subject is correctly focused. Now you can fully depress the release and take the shot. If you depress the release before this indicator lights up no exposure will be made.

As the green in-focus LED only lights up when the image is in sharp focus, and the release can only then be triggered, it follows that unsharp pictures are practically impossible with the F-401. Even if the lighting conditions are too poor for the autofocus to work, or the subject lacks sufficient contrast or is too confusing, or the attached lens is not an AF-system lens, the release will be blocked. In such cases the green in-focus LED in the viewfinder will blink, indicating that the image cannot be focused automatically.

Focusing with the Main Subject Off-centre

An off-centre main subject presents no problem. You start, as usual, by bringing the main subject within the focusing field at the centre of the viewfinder. Then you depress the release to first pressure position and allow the autofocus to operate. As soon as the green in-focus indicator lights up in the viewfinder you re-align the camera to select the framing that you actually want. The release is kept lightly depressed all this time, which keeps the focus in memory and set on the lens, until you finally depress it fully to take the shot. Should you decide not to make the exposure after all then this is no problem either. Simply take your finger off the release button and the stored setting will be cancelled. Now you are free to focus on a new subject, depressing the release again to initiate a new focusing sequence. The explanations here may sound complicated, but the actions involved are really very simple and should soon become second nature.

The AF mechanism is even suited to relatively fast shots. To get a fast shot, point the camera, as usual, at the main subject and fully depress the release, the exposure will then be made without delay as soon as the AF mechanism has focused. This process could take as long as a second, depending on subject contrast, brightness, distance and lens attached, but in the ideal case it could take as little as a fifth of a second. Moving subjects too, can be "caught" quite easily by using this method of fully depressed release. This has the added advantage that the exposure will be taken at exactly the moment when focusing has been achieved and not slightly later. This means that you could be faster with the autofocus than an experienced sports photographer with manual focusing. The only problem with moving subjects is that they move relatively fast across the field of view and are soon lost from the centre of the screen. You could get many unwanted, but sharply focused, shots with this method of fully-depressed release.

Self-timer and Autofocus

The self-timer has predominance over the autofocus in the F-401. Once the self-timer button is depressed, the red LED indicator on the front of the camera will blink and the release will be automatically triggered after about 10 seconds, *without* activating the autofocus mechanism. However, the exposure mechanism remains fully functional in the self-timer sequence.

To use the self-timer you proceed as follows: aim at the main subject from the position from where you wish to take the shot, and focus by using the autofocus mechanism, keeping the release depressed to first pressure position. Then take the pressure off the release button and press the self-timer button (be careful not to depress the self-timer twice, as the second pressure cancels the self-timer sequence!). The camera will now release with the last memorized focusing setting.

For shots with the self-timer then:

○ First focus by AF or manually.
○ Then depress self-timer button.

Autofocus is Not Suitable for Every Subject

Extremely fast-moving subjects are not particularly suitable for AF shooting. Just imagine the situation where a cyclist is racing towards you. With the method described above of keeping the release button fully depressed, you will get the cyclist sharply into the picture only by pure accident. The release will more often than not be blocked, or it will release on the perfectly-focused background. In such cases it is better to set the shooting mode selector to **M** (manual focusing). In the manual focusing mode you still have the electronic focus-aid facility to assist you in accurate focusing.

To use this mode, focus the lens to the distance at which you wish to take the subject and depress the release to first pressure position. Now you have to wait for the moving subject to pass through your preset distance of sharpness. As soon as the subject is in focus the green LED will light up and you can depress the release fully; the subject being "trapped" in the AF focusing range.

Limits of Autofocus

The method for distance metering used by the AF mechanism is passive. This means that the sharpness of the subject is assessed at the image as projected by the lens. The required adjustment of the lens is calculated by the AF-minicomputer. In order for the autofocus to work, the subject has to possess a certain minimum contrast, and the image produced by the subject through the camera's lens must not be too dark. The following requirements can be summarized for proper functioning of the AF function:

- ○ a clearly-defined subject
- ○ sufficient subject contrast
- ○ sufficient subject brightness
- ○ sufficient lens speed.

Let us first consider the lens speed. The Nikon AF lenses have a lens speed of at least f/5.6. The AF mechanism could not function for lens speeds slower than this, i.e. f/8 or f/11. This will not apply to AF lenses as they have been designed with these constraints in mind. But if you are using some other Nikon lens, which is quite likely as it is one of the advantages of the new AF-camera, you have to ensure that its maximum aperture is big enough. If you wish to make use of the focusing aid in manual focus mode **M**, then this will not be possible with f/5.6 or slower lenses. The camera indicates this by the flashing green in-focus indicator in the viewfinder. It is still possible to use such a lens, but focusing has to be done completely unaided on the focusing screen, as in the good old days. This is not a very important point as you should use only the new AF lenses with the F-401. The autofocus does not work with any other lens, and, more importantly, the exposure metering will also not function.

Dimly-lit subjects are also critical, but don't worry unduly. I was able to take successful shots with the F-401 with very dim subjects where it was even difficult to focus manually. Nikon have devised a sophisticated and highly sensitive AF-metering mechanism which allows reliable focusing even with subjects with an exposure value (EV) of only 2. EV2 would correspond to a room of about 10 square metres, or about 100 sq.feet, lit by a 40W to 60W tungsten ceiling light. But not only is the level of illumination important, the subject must also be uniformly lit. After all, the AF system only measures the centre part of the frame, and if the main subject is hidden in a dark corner, even the highly-sensitive AF mechanism cannot cope. The only solution in these situations is manual focusing. In emergencies you will have to judge the distance and make an approximate setting. If you are lucky enough to possess the AF flashgun SB-20, or the SB-22, then you can use the infrared flash to focus.

Subjects with poor contrast are another source of problems to the automatic focusing facility. By contrast we mean that the subject has to have dark and bright areas and that these areas have clearly defined boundaries. Just try and focus on a smooth white wall. The autofocus will adjust the lens from close-up to infinity and then the green in-focus indicator will flash, telling you that it cannot focus. Another problem subject is one with a profusion of fine contrasty lines, for example, print on a newspaper. Whether this will work or not will depends on the reproduction ratio. Horizontal lines are also not particularly favoured by the AF mechanism. This is because the sensors are aligned to vertical structures, although the F-401 copes better in this respect that the earlier F-501. Even so, there is an easy way out. Simply turn the camera to the vertical position, take the distance setting, keep the finger on the release to hold it, re-align the camera for the required framing and take the picture.

Extreme backlit subjects and excessively-reflective surfaces could also cause problems because light scatter in the AF target field can reduce the contrast to an inadmissible degree. However, this is rarely the case.

Lastly we have to consider subjects with confusing spatial relationships. By this I mean, for example, subjects that are staggered in space in a complicated array. Imagine two children, one standing behind the other. Part of the face of the farthest child and part of the nearer child are within the target field. Which child should the autofocus choose? In my experience so far I have found that the focusing system tends to select the closer subject. This preference could be annoying if you tried to take a shot through a fence, or the bars of a cage, where you do not want the sharp outlines of the metal. In such cases it would be necessary to ensure that the important subject detail is placed within the target field, excluding the confusing foreground. With the focusing setting stored, the camera can then be re-aligned to take the shot for the required framing. If this is unsuccessful, then there is always manual focusing.

I hope my description of unsuitable subjects for the AF function will not make you doubt its usefulness and reliability. May I allay your doubts by pointing out that in my experience

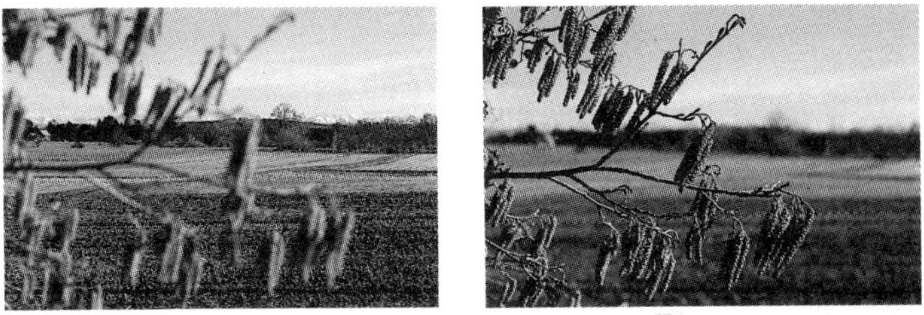

The autofocus will not know which is the main subject to focus on; is it the foreground or the background? Whenever the foreground is in the AF metering field, the AF function will normally choose the foreground because it usually has higher contrast.

I found the AF mechanism more sensitive than the human eye. We can discern subjects only if it is light enough and the details and outlines are sufficiently defined. My own experience has shown that the focusing limitations of the F-401 are approximately those of the human eye.

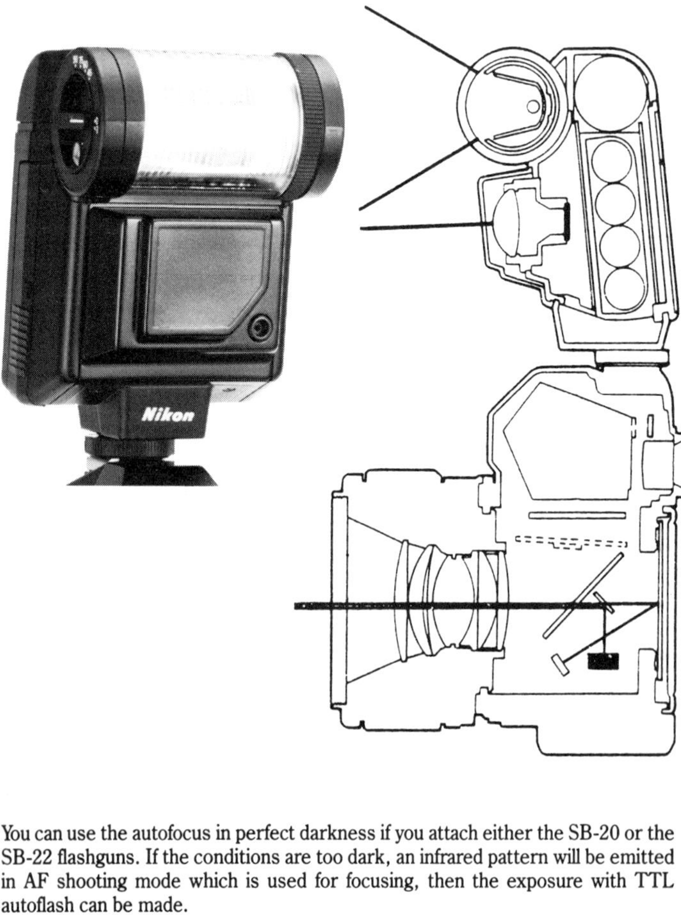

You can use the autofocus in perfect darkness if you attach either the SB-20 or the SB-22 flashguns. If the conditions are too dark, an infrared pattern will be emitted in AF shooting mode which is used for focusing, then the exposure with TTL autoflash can be made.

Automatic Focusing in the Dark

There are situations where not only the autofocus goes on strike, but also the human eye. The autofocus flash SB-20 or SB-22 has the answer! This flashgun has an additional special AF infrared flash in addition to the normal flash functions. This means that if the F-401 is set to AF focus mode **A** and you depress the release button, the AF flash will send out an infrared flash to light the subject if the lighting conditions are insufficient for the AF mechanism to take a reading. This AF flash will be prolonged until the AF has obtained a satisfactory setting. This arrangement guarantees a sharp flash picture. If you do not wish to expose with the flash you can switch the flashgun off, always keeping the finger on the release to retain the AF setting. Moreover, you could then change to manual focus mode **M** and use the stored AF setting to take the most beautiful available light shots in any exposure mode that seems appropriate for the subject. The AF flash focusing method has further advantages.

The focusing flash projects a vertical striped pattern and is therefore useful for taking readings of subjects of low contrast. You may consider this facility totally useless, as you cannot see much in total or near-total darkness. Not so, the IR focusing light includes visible red light and the focusing flashes – impulses to be precise – are long enough to be clearly visible in the dark. Up to 5m away you can make out the object you are focusing on quite clearly. To assess the situation you should not look through the viewfinder but directly at the subject.

Manual Focusing in Emergency

For subjects that are unsuitable for automatic focusing, or if you are using a lens that cannot be used in AF mode, then you will have to focus manually. The optical path to the focusing screen is equivalent to the path of the light when it meets the film plane with the mirror folded away. The sharpness on the focusing screen is therefore an excellent indication of whether the subject has been properly focused or not. In principle, a normal focusing screen should be quite adequate. It only needs to be sufficiently fine and uniformly grained. The focusing screen of the F-401 is just that. That the focusing screen has no focusing aids, such as a crossed prism indicator or microprism ring, is more of an advantage than a disadvantage. These focusing aids tend to darken when used with long-focus or with slow lenses and that makes focusing more difficult rather than easier. The focusing screen fitted as standard in the F-401 is straightforward. It is possible to focus even in failing light and using a 500mm f/8 telephoto lens. If your eyesight is good, or you are wearing suitable glasses, then manual focusing is still possible, even if the autofocus is for some reason unable to operate.

Whether the supplementary eyepiece lens is a useful accessory is questionable in view of the autofocus facility. On the other hand the eyecup and the various correction lenses are useful accessories. If you find it difficult to see the viewfinder display with your glasses or contact lenses, then you can get the appropriate correction lens to suit your eyesight. They are available from Nikon in strengths of −5, −4, −3, −2, −1, +0.5, +1, +2 and +3 dioptres.

This is how fast the autofocus works: these cars were travelling at about 50 mph and were taken at the 200mm setting on the AF Zoom 70-210mm, f/4.0 from a distance of about 50m (sequence of shots from top left to bottom right). This was the fastest sequence as the camera releases only after perfect focus has been obtained. Manual presetting on a given distance might have been faster. *Photo: Michael Huber*

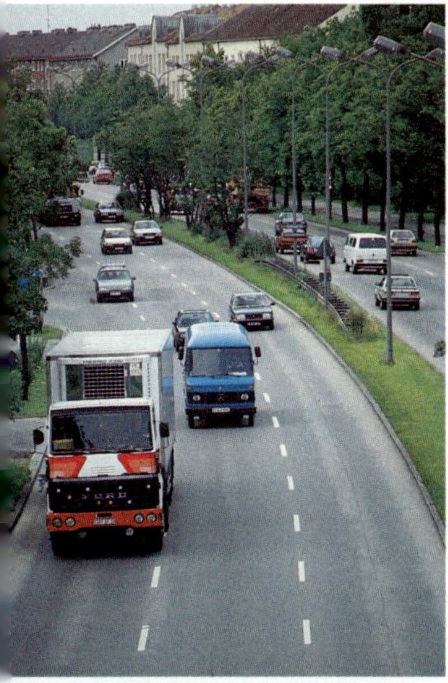

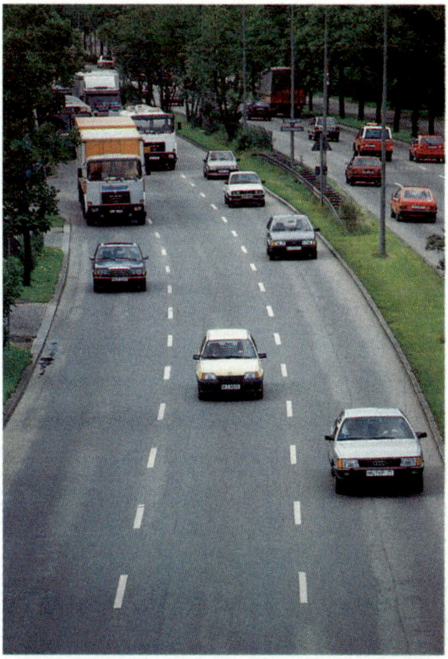

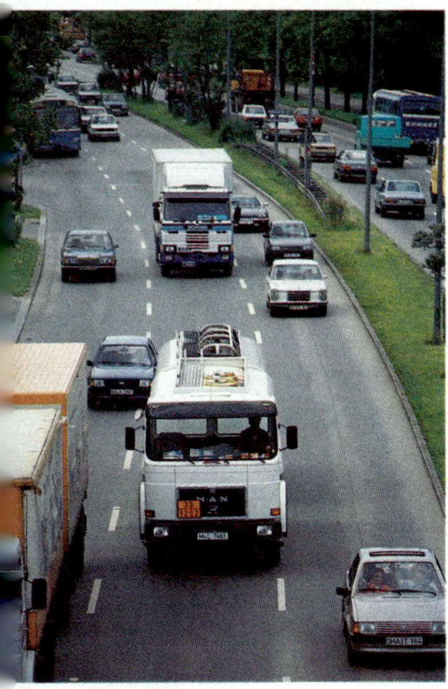

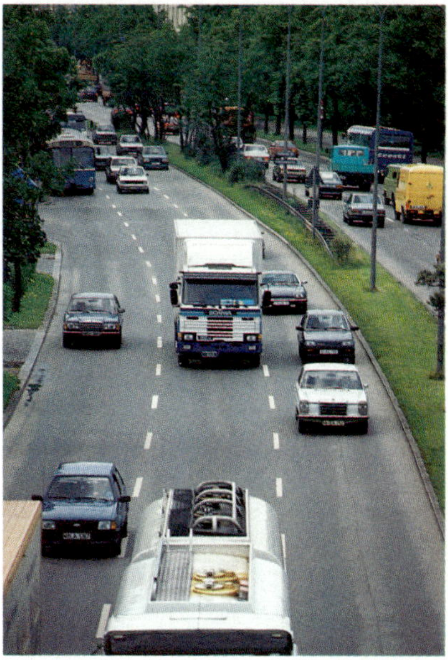

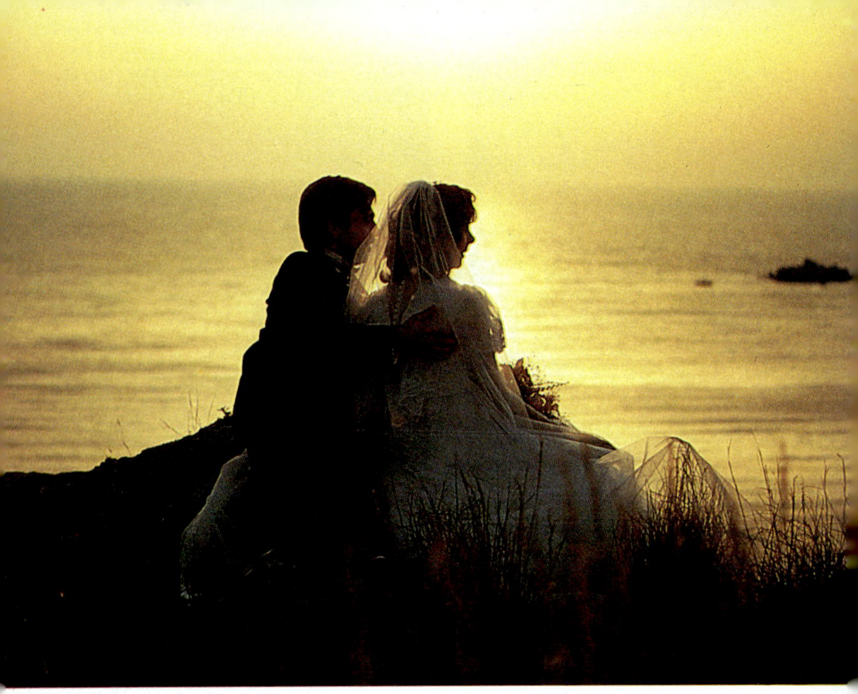

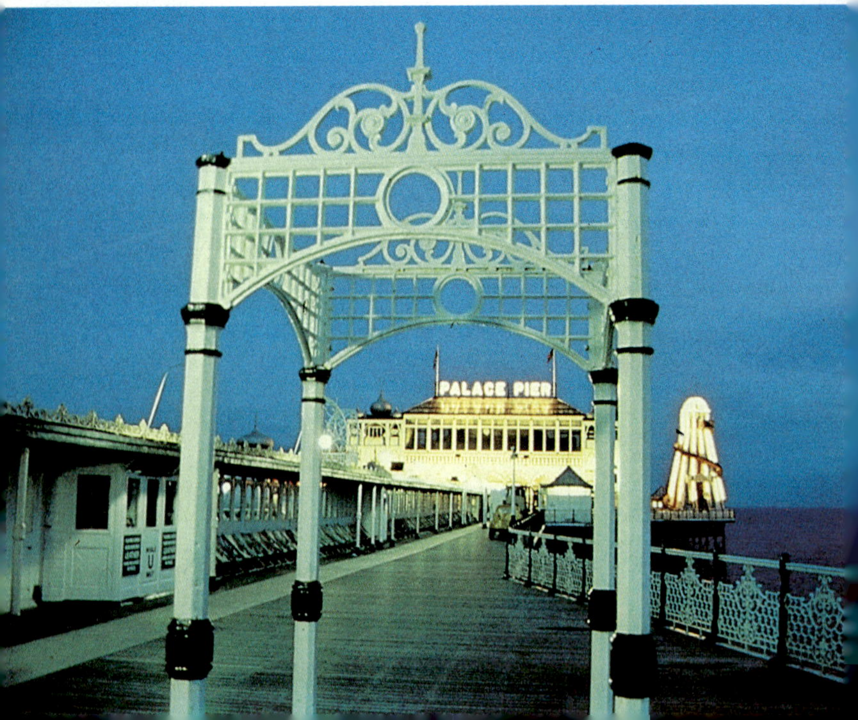
PALACE PIER

This is How the Autofocus Works

The AF mechanism of the F-401 consists basically of four modules. The first is the microcomputer in the lens. This conveys the typical characteristic values such as lens speed (maximum aperture), focal length and focusing distance via the AF contacts in the bayonet to the camera. Within the camera there is the AF distance metering unit (AF-Focus-IC). This consists of an image converter using CCD semi-conductor technology with 200 metering fields. The metering signals from these CCD units are interpreted by a special integrated circuit (IC) and the result is passed to the central microcomputer (CPU) in the camera. The data supplied by the metering unit and those from the lens are combined in the CPU and converted into the appropriate command for focus setting. This instruction is conveyed to the AF servo motor unit. The AF motor drive IC converts these instructions into numbers of revolutions and triggers the motor to turn this exact number of revolutions in a forward or backward direction. A light barrier with an interrupt disc counts the motor revolutions and reports them back to the AF motor IC. The revolutions of the AF motor are transmitted via a gear train and coupling to the lens gear which performs the exact number of revolutions for distance setting of the lens. As soon as the lens setting is completed the CPU requests a further sharpness reading from the distance metering IC and, if appropriate, passes the message "in-focus" to the IC

This composition of the bride and groom was very beautifully set against the sunset. The view below of the pier was taken shortly after sunset. The blue residual light and the mixture of yellow tungsten light make an interesting colour composition. *Photos: Wolf Huber*

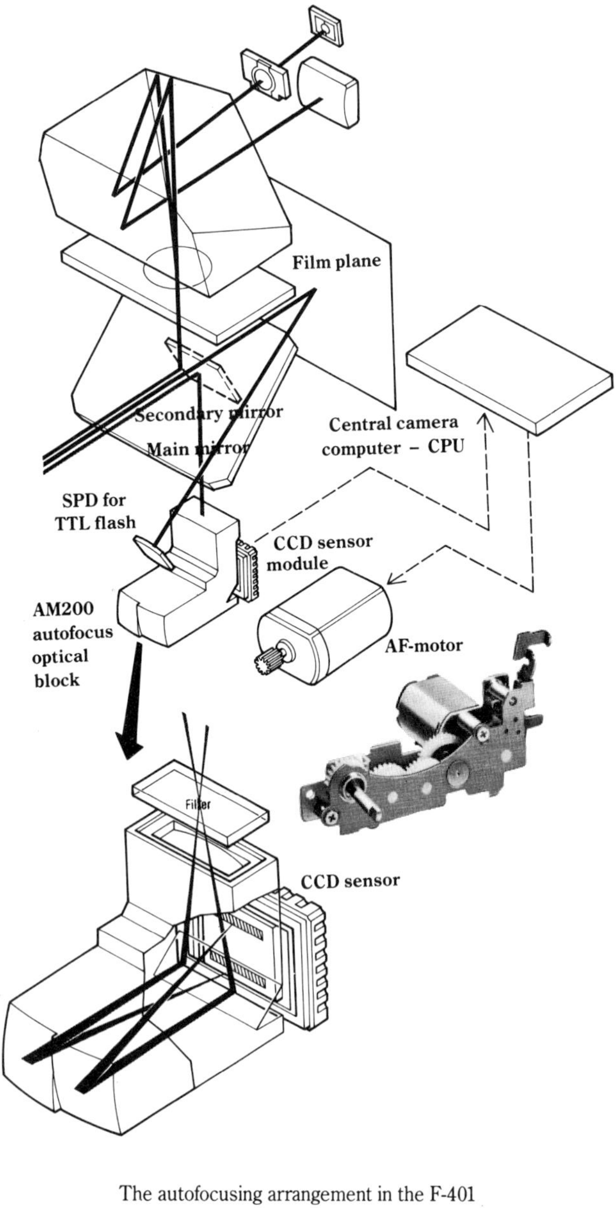

The autofocusing arrangement in the F-401

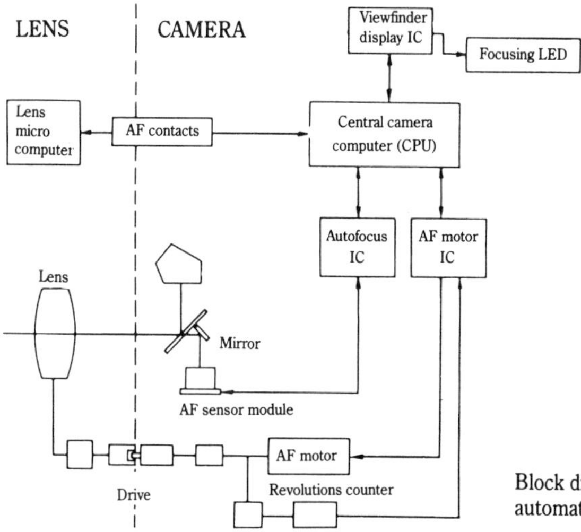

Block diagram showing automatic focusing

in the viewfinder. Now the green in-focus LED in the viewfinder will light up. Under ideal circumstances the whole process from measuring to completed focusing could take as little as a tenth of a second.

If the distance metering IC reports incorrect focusing to the CPU after the lens had been adjusted, which could be the case in poor lighting conditions or for poorly-defined subjects, then the focusing process is repeated by moving the lens through the distance settings from close-up to infinity. If this is unsuccessful then the CPU reports to the viewfinder display by the flashing of the green in-focus LED that focusing cannot be effected.

To understand how the electronic distance metering, or recognition of sharpness, functions in the F-401 we first have to define what sharpness is. A lens is set to the correct distance if every point of a subject for that distance is represented as a sharp point on the film plane in the camera. If the distance is not correctly set, then the point will no longer be sharply defined, it begins to get bigger and flow into other image points around it.

There are two situations of unsharpness. Setting for too

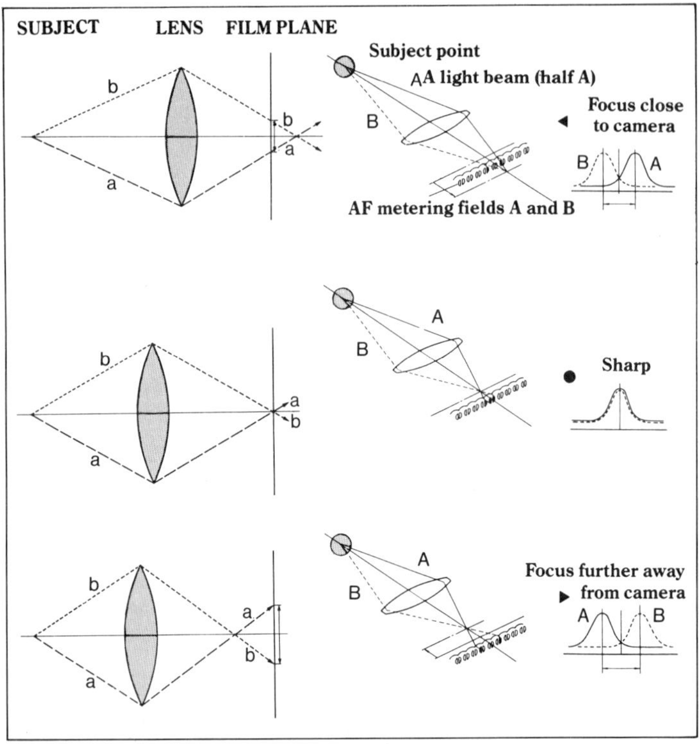

The camera computer recognises by the phase shift the amount and direction of focusing movement.

close or setting for too far. For example, if the subject is 5m distant from the lens, but the lens is set at 2m, then the light rays from a certain subject point would combine in front of the film plane. To obtain sharp focus the lens would have to be turned in the direction of 5m (this is clockwise in the case of Nikon lenses) until the light rays combined exactly on the film plane. On the other hand, if the subject was 5m distant, but the lens was set to infinity, then the light rays would combine behind the film plane. The lens now has to be turned in counter-clockwise direction towards 5m.

The distance metering mechanism in the AF system of the

F-401 has the task of measuring and assessing the blurring of unsharp pictures, so that the direction in which the lens will have to be turned can be ascertained. The microcomputer in the camera can then calculate the required distance the lens has to be turned to obtain correct focus. To do this the sensor unit (CCD-Chip + evaluation IC) measures the expansion of the image point on the film plane due to incorrect focusing. To be precise, the measurement is not taken on the film plane; part of the light is allowed to pass through the partially-translucent mirror and this is projected towards the CCD-chip, the length of the path for this portion of light is exactly the same as that to the film plane. The trick employed by the AF system is that it consists of two types of metering fields. Type A and type B. A facetted lens is placed in front of each of these measuring pairs, A and B, so that the light beam emitted from the subject point and passed through the lens is split and combined at metering points for each lens half. Let's consider the simplest case with the lens set to the correct focusing distance. In this case the light beam of the sharp image point is projected onto the AF sensor such that the two adjacent metering fields comprise practically the entire light beam. Metering field A receives the light from one half of the lens, metering field B receives the light from the other half. The electronic evaluation circuits in the focusing-IC compare the two measured curves of measuring points A and B. If the two curves coincide, or to use an electronics term: if the curves are in phase, then the focusing-IC reports to the microcomputer "image in focus".

Now consider the case when the lens is set too close and the unsharp image lies in front of the film plane. In this case the blurred image point in the AF sensor illuminates not just one measuring pair, but a whole sequence. As a result, the two measuring curves A and B (to be precise the curves of A-measuring field and B-measuring field) diverge at the maximum points.

The same occurs when the lens is set for too great a distance: the two measuring curves will also diverge, i.e.

they are not in phase. But the direction of the divergence for "too close" is opposite to that for for "too far" and the focusing-IC recognises immediately in what direction the lens has to be turned. This information is transferred to the central microcomputer in the camera. The focusing-IC also interprets by way of this phase detection how far the curves are offset or divergent from each other. This provides the measure of how far the lens has to be turned to obtain maximum sharpness. This information is also conveyed to the CPU, and the camera calculates from this information together with the lens data the required lens settings.

Who guards whom? An interesting shot taken with a 35mm lens. In situations such as these the autofocus could easily be confused. Normally it would focus on the fence. If the main subject were standing further back from the fence he could have been unsharp if the depth of field was insufficient. So focus manually and keep the depth of field within precisely defined limits by selecting a suitable aperture in aperture priority mode. Photo: Rudolf Dietrich

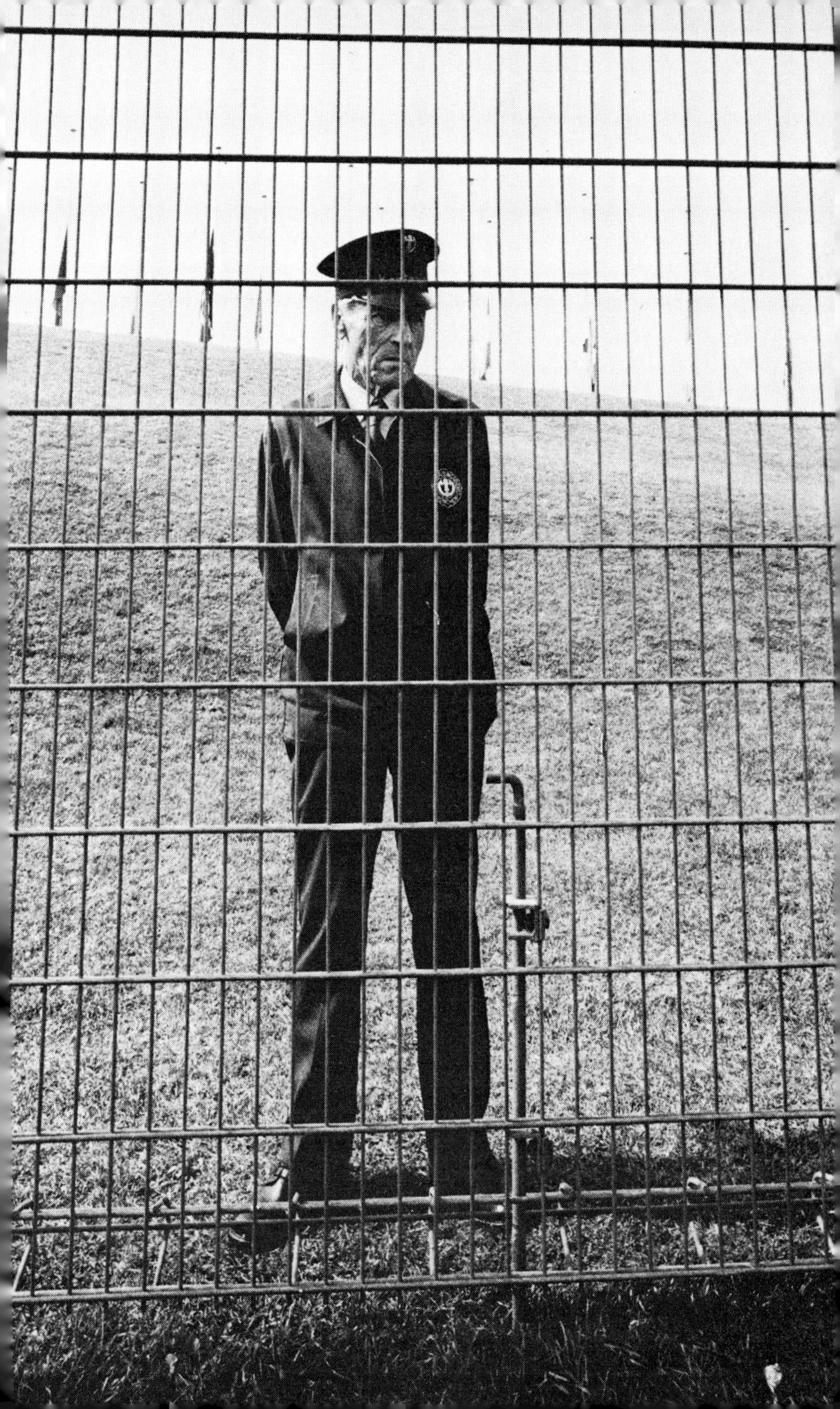

Fully Automatic Shooting in Program Mode

In the program mode your camera will select the correct aperture and shutter speed, depending on the amount of light and the film speed. The only thing that the photographer has to do, provided the autofocus facility is also selected, is point at the subject and select the required framing. Even if a longer focal length has been selected, the Image Master Control System of the F-401 will recognize this fact and change the standard program to the high-speed program with focal lengths from 135mm upwards. The F-401 functions completely automatically when set to Program Auto Exposure Mode.

Using Program Auto Exposure Mode

After loading the film, setting the shutter speed dial to **A**, and the aperture selector dial to **S**, you can start. If you now look through the viewfinder and lightly depress the release, the

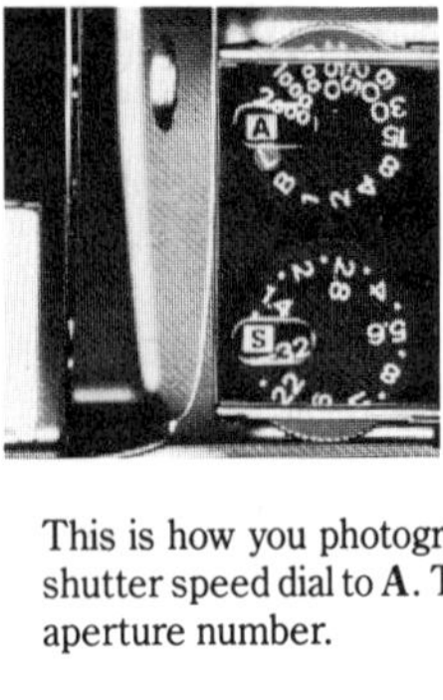

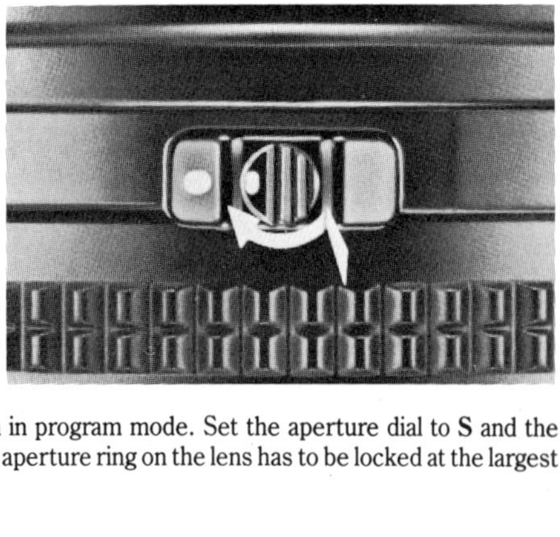

This is how you photograph in program mode. Set the aperture dial to **S** and the shutter speed dial to **A**. The aperture ring on the lens has to be locked at the largest aperture number.

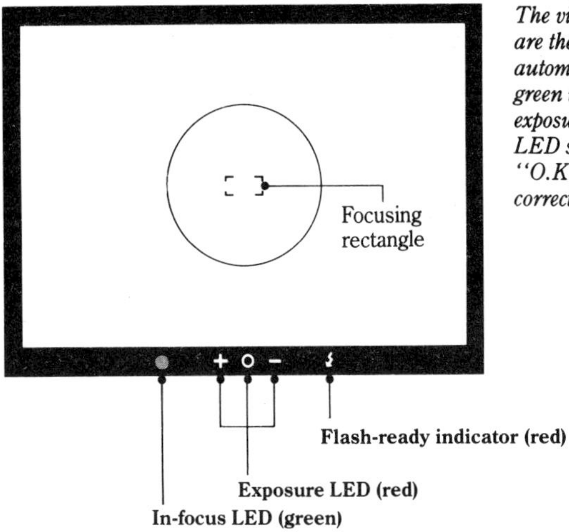

The viewfinder displays are the same in all automatic modes. The green in-focus LED, exposure LEDs and flash LED signal either "O.K." or indicates corrective measures.

exposure metering sequence is activated. If the red circular LED lights up at the centre of the small display panel in the viewfinder, then the conditions are satisfactory. You need not make any more adjustments and can, provided the autofocus has focused correctly, take the shot. It is not even necessary to check in the viewfinder if everything is OK. The release will be blocked by the Image Master Control System should the readings indicate incorrect exposure. One glance in the viewfinder will inform you then of the reason: if the red plus LED lights up, then this means that the conditions are too bright, i.e. for the speed of the film loaded in the camera, with even the smallest aperture and fastest shutter speed, overexposure is unavoidable. Similarly, if the red minus LED lights up, underexposure is indicated, i.e. the subject brightness is insufficient even with the largest aperture. In the latter case the red flash symbol will also blink, reminding you to use the integrated flash. If the brightness of the integrated flash is also insufficient to cope with the situation, then you could use an additional flash that has to be inserted in the accessory shoe.

If the minus LED and the plus LED light up alternately, then this indicates that you have forgotten to set the aperture of your Nikon AF lens to the largest aperture number (smallest aperture) and locked it in this position.

When the red exposure LED indicator flashes, then you are reminded that the shutter speed calculated by the camera computer is $^1/_{30}$ sec. or slower, and camera shake is likely. In this case you should activate the integrated flash or set the camera on a tripod. Another possibility is to change to shutter speed priority mode. In this mode you can select a suitable shutter speed of $^1/_{60}$ sec. or faster and the camera will select the appropriate aperture, provided the lens can offer aperture values of f/2 or f/1.4.

For program mode, as for all other automatic shooting modes of the F-401, it is important to ensure that the lens used has the necessary aperture value transfer facilities. From the Nikon lenses listed in the table in this book only the AF lenses marked with an asterisk have this facility.

Suitable Films and Lenses for Program Mode

Before we think about which subjects are best suited to the program modes I would like to make some suggestions on the choice of films and lenses:

- ○ The most suitable lenses range from a 28mm wide-angle to 200mm telephoto lenses; this corresponds to the range of the most popular zoom lenses.
- ○ For the general program the most suitable films are ISO 100 to 200.
- ○ For moving subjects, I would recommend the faster ISO 400 films for colour slide and also for colour print photography. In this case the shutter speed priority mode may be the better.

Program Mode for Snapshots and the Family Album

The program mode is perfect for family snapshots, such as children, friends, pets, and for holiday mementoes – street scenes, beach scenes, landscapes, etc. In this shooting mode you need not worry about aperture or shutter speed settings and can concentrate fully on your subject. This type of photography is often looked down on as simple "snapshot photography", but it need not be such a negative concept. Natural expressions, unrehearsed scenes, the fleeting moment caught, all of these presuppose that the photographer acted quickly, without first having to fumble awkwardly with light meter and aperture and shutter speed settings. It is quite obvious that not every situation and subject is suitable for this snapshot technique. Pure landscape photographs, for example, will be properly exposed in program mode, but you could encounter some problems with regard to depth of field. If you need to show everything in sharp focus, from close-up to infinity, then you are better served in aperture priority mode. You can then select f/16, which will give you greater depth of field than f/4, and the camera will do the rest. To obtain small enough aperture openings in program mode, the subject brightness and film speed have to be quite high and this will not always be the case. The aperture priority mode is obviously the ideal mode for creative picture control through depth of field and you should select this mode on the F-401.

Moving subjects, for example in sports photography, are generally not very well suited for the program mode. The preselected shutter speeds are generally too slow for this purpose. Moreover, if you are also using one of the longer focal length lenses, as is normally required to get a close view of the subject, then the danger of camera-shake is added to movement blur. You may know this already, but the shutter speed should not exceed the reciprocal of the focal length of the lens in mm to avoid camera-shake. This means that for a 500mm lens, the shutter speed should not be slower than $^1/_{500}$ sec. to be reasonably sure that the shot will not be blurred due to camera movement. To ensure that the shutter speed is not slower than $^1/_{250}$ sec. in the high-speed program mode, you have to load a rather fast film of ISO 400 or faster. However, if you are using shutter speed priority mode and a reasonably fast telephoto lens, an ISO 400 film should be sufficient. The limits of program mode are defined by particular requirements with regard to depth of field on the one hand, and by fast shutter speeds for moving subjects on the other.

How Program Mode Works

The program mode calculates the exposure value from the subject brightness and the set film speed. The result is automatically converted into the appropriate combination of aperture value and shutter speed by the program curve. The program will select from all the possible exposure time/ aperture combinations the one that corresponds best with the normal program or the high speed program curve. These are represented by the program curves of the F-401.

But what happens if the iris diaphragm sticks, or if it is too loose? In such a situation the selected aperture would not agree with the calculated value and using the program mode would be a risky business. And what happens when the calculated aperture value is not available on the lens used? A lens with a largest opening of f/4 cannot be set to f/2.8 let alone f/2, even if the program curve decided that this was the best value. This problem has been solved rather well by Nikon. After depressing the shutter release and after the aperture has been closed to the selected value, the actual subject brightness is re-measured at the last moment, just before the mirror springs up, and this value is used for the final calculation of the shutter speed. The actual exposure will therefore correspond to the aperture/shutter speed combination of the program curve only in the ideal case. Only the final measurement of subject brightness at closed aperture, taken some milliseconds before actual exposure, serves for the final calculation and setting of the shutter speed. This has the advantage that, irrespective of any mechanical inaccuracy of the diaphragm mechanism and errors in transferring aperture data, the exposure should always be correct. If you are working with zoom lenses, which have no uniform lens speed (e.g. the AF Nikkor 35-70mm,f3.3-4.5 Zoom), you will encounter no problems with the program mode. If it has calculated the aperture as f/3.3 and the shutter speed as 1/300 sec. from the subject brightness and film speed, then the actual aperture will be slightly larger, depending on the focal length selected on the zoom. This will have no effect on the correct exposure as the final measurement with closed aperture will cause the exposure time to be lengthened as appropriate.

If we examine the diagram of the program curves we note that this is an exposure value/aperture/time curve. In order to interpret this it is necessary to understand what is meant by exposure value. Regardless of whether you use a Nikon or any other camera, you will find that most modern camera manufacturers use this term to define the measuring range of their cameras. The exposure value (EV) is a quantity denoting a number of equivalent aperture/shutter speed combinations. Equivalent here means that these combinations will all produce the same effect with regard to exposure. Examples of aperture/shutter speed combinations are given here: –

The following combinations correspond to EV8

Aperture	32	22	16	11	8	5.6	4	2.8	2	1.4
Speed (sec)	4	2	1	1/2	1/4	1/8	1/15	1/30	1/60	1/125

The following correspond to EV12

Aperture	32	22	16	11	8	5.6	4	2.8	2	1.4
Speed (sec)	1/4	1/8	1/15	1/30	1/60	1/125	1/250	1/500	1/1000	1/2000

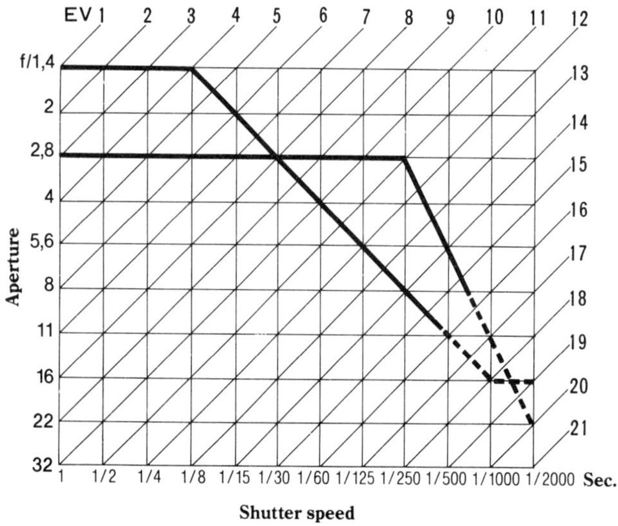

The program curve of the F-401. The F-401 will automatically switch between high speed and normal programs. The high speed curve starts with EV3 at aperture f/2.8 and 1 sec. and works from EV8 with relatively large apertures in favour of faster shutter speeds. This corresponds to the requirements when longer focal length lenses are used. The normal program curve starts at EV1 with aperture f/1.4 and 1 sec. It favours smaller apertures and slower shutter speeds, and from EV8 it is better suited to the shorter focal length lenses.

The following correspond to EV17					
Aperture	32	22	16	11	8
Speed (sec)	1/125	1/250	1/500	1/1000	1/2000

A difference of one EV corresponds to a difference in exposure of one stop, or a doubling or halving of the exposure time as the case may be.

If we now apply this to the program curve we will observe the following. If the measurement of the subject brightness with film speed ISO 100 produces an exposure value of 7, which would probably be the case for an indoor photograph in a room lit by artificial light, then the high speed program would select an aperture of f/2.8 and provisionally choose a shutter speed of 1/15 sec. If the camera measures EV12, which might be the case for an outdoor picture with heavy cloud cover and using an ISO 100 film, the camera would select, in high speed program mode, an aperture of f/2.8/4 and a shutter speed of about $^1/_{300}$ sec. If the measurement produces an exposure value of EV17, for example an outdoor situation with cloudless sky, bright sunshine and an ISO 400 film, then the high-speed program would always select an aperture of f/11 and a shutter speed of $^1/_{1000}$ sec.

In normal program mode the situation is similar, only now the program will favour slower shutter speeds with larger apertures. An exposure value of 7 would result in an aperture of f/2/2.8 and a shutter speed of about $^1/_{20}$ sec. For EV12 the aperture has to be stopped down to f/5.6 and the shutter speed reduced to $^1/_{125}$ sec.

What range of the program mode curve the camera selects depends on the film speed. If the measured exposure value is, for example, 8 and the film speed ISO 50, then the çamera will automatically select an aperture of f/2.8 and a shutter speed of $^1/_{30}$ sec. If, however, an ISO 400 film is used for the same subject brightness, then the measured exposure value will be 11. In normal program the camera will now select an aperture of f/4/5.6 and the shutter speed will be reduced to $^1/_{60}$ sec.

Limits of Program Mode

Let us have a closer look at the normal program. We find that if we are using a lens with a speed of f/1.4 it will behave like an aperture-priority program for calculated exposure value EV1 (aperture f/1.4 and 1 sec.), i.e. the aperture remains the same, the exposure is controlled by varying the shutter speed. In the case of the high speed program this range extends from EV3 (aperture f/2.8 and 1 sec.) to EV11 (aperture f/2.8 and $^1/_{250}$ sec.). From EV18 (aperture f/16 and $^1/_{1000}$ sec.) the normal program changes over to aperture priority and ends with EV19 (aperture f/16 and $^1/_{2000}$ sec.).

The reason that the normal program stops at a smallest aperture opening of f/16 may be attributed to the fact that most lenses with short or medium focal lengths usually have no smaller aperture opening than f/16.

The exposure curve of the high speed program extends to EV20 (aperture f/22 with $^{1}/_{2000}$ sec.). According to my own tests, however, it will extend to EV21 if the attached lens can be stopped down to f/32 (aperture f/32 and $^{1}/_{2000}$ sec.).

Whenever the program mode bases its decisions on the triple sensor light metering, which is always the case when the exposure memory lock is not used, then the normal and the high speed program ends at exposure value $15^{2}/_{3}$. For this reason the program curves are continued from this point by broken lines. The unbroken lines correspond to the values when an ISO 100 film is loaded. For faster films, the program curves will continue along the broken lines. There are other reasons for restricting the curves to these ranges. Exposure values higher than EV16 are very rare for subjects with normal reflectivity in normal lighting conditions. If we take the case of a white sandy beach or a snowscape in bright sunlight, and an ISO 100 film in the camera, then we have a situation where the exposure value would rise beyond EV16. If the exposure control now underexposes the scene to compensate for the extremely light subject, then the light sand or the white snow would appear dirty-grey in the final photograph. The Image Master Control automatically increases exposures for such subjects, just as a good photographer would, by employing manual exposure correction.

The impact of this photograph is not only due to the typical wide-angle perspective. The large grain and the slight diffusion, generally unwelcome effects, contribute here to the special impression. The recipe is relatively coarse-grain film (e.g. ORWO UT21), diffuser and slight underexposure. To obtain the balance of brightness and colour the original slide was duplicated.
Photo: Wolf Huber

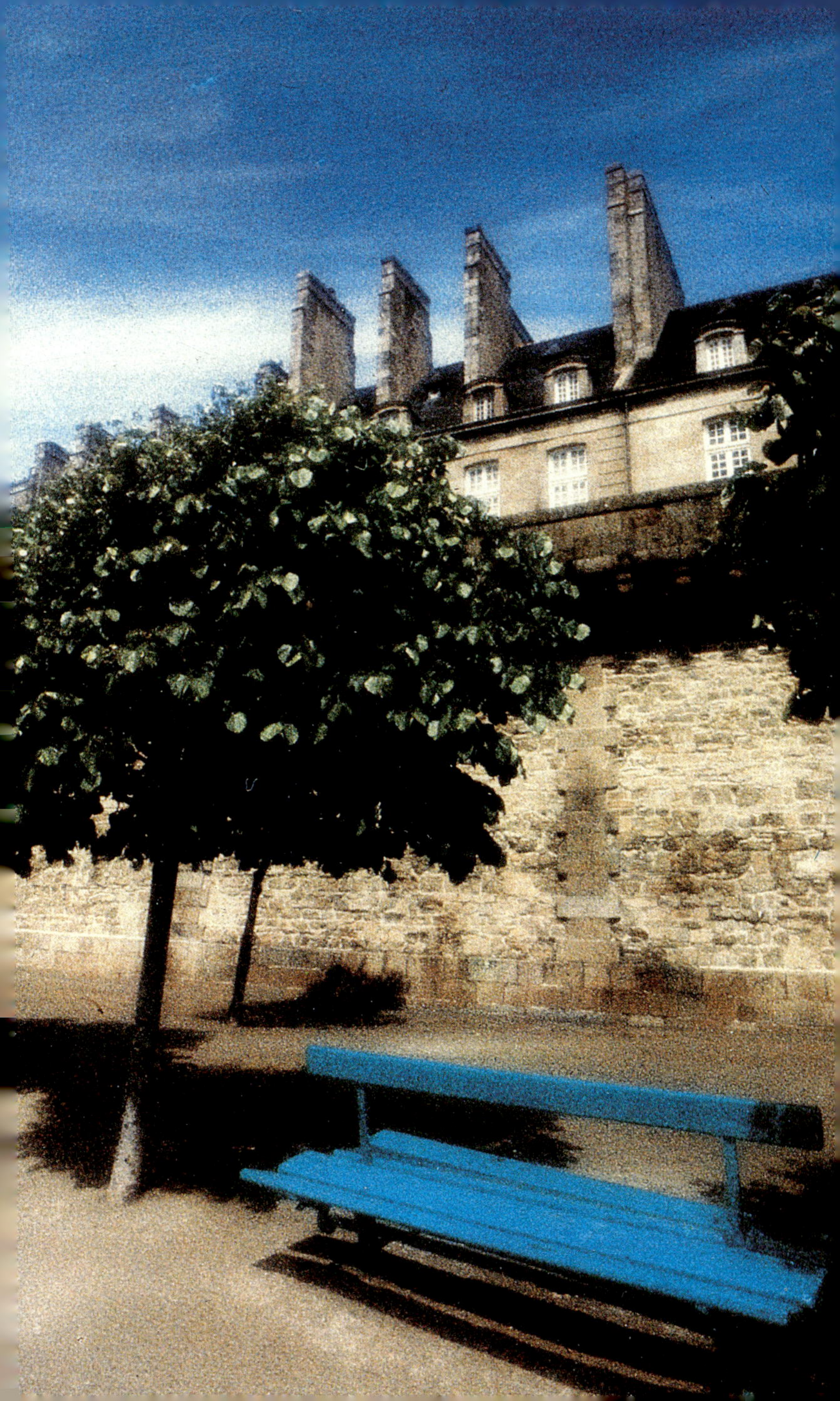

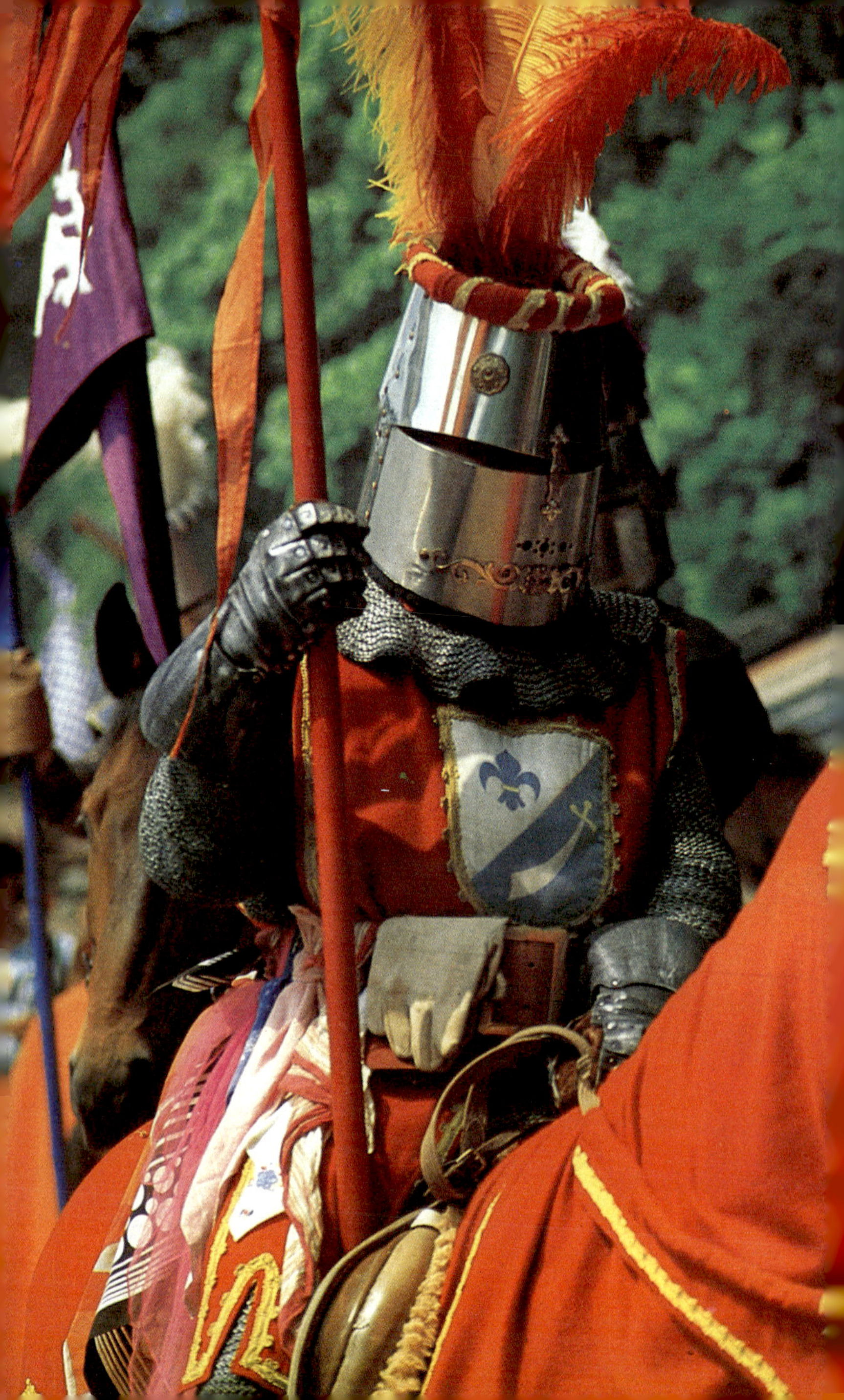

As mentioned previously, the program mode re-checks the brightness levels for the chosen aperture. This means that after the aperture is closed to the value calculated by the program, the subject brightness is measured again and the actual valid exposure time is calculated and automatically selected. The actual speed of the shutter is thus perhaps a little slower or faster. The program curves are therefore somewhat more flexible than shown. To be precise, the program modes are shutter speed priority modes with subsequent aperture priority mode. However, as the aperture priority has the real priority, the F-401 actually attains great accuracy in the program modes and is very reliable in producing correct exposure levels.

The above fact has a positive effect if you are using a lens which is not as fast as the largest value on the program curve of the normal program – i.e. if the largest value is, say, only f/2.8. For an exposure value of EV6, for example, the normal program can no longer select f/2 and $^1/_{15}$ sec. In this case the aperture stays fully open at f/2.8 and the program will, after final measurement, adjust the shutter speed to $^1/_8$ sec., which will produce the correct exposure level. The actual range of the normal program mode for a lens with a speed of f/2.8 maximum aperture therefore does not start with EV4 (aperture f/1.4 and $^1/_8$ sec.), but only EV8 (aperture f/2.8 and $^1/_{30}$ sec.).

In the program mode you can use only lenses with electronic data transfer with the F-401. Lenses with fixed apertures, and those which allow no transfer of aperture data, are not compatible. This restriction applies not only to the program modes, but to all exposure modes of the F-401. Please read the appropriate chapters on lenses in this book!

This colourful knight is just a lucky shot. Taken in program mode and with the zoom lens set at 200mm. *Photo: Wolf Huber*

Shutter Speed Priority for Sport and Action

In this mode the photographer chooses a shutter speed and the camera will automatically select a suitable aperture for the subject brightness and film speed. This exposure mode is useful whenever the shutter speed is of importance and the aperture can take second place in image creation. This will often be the case when moving subjects are taken or long focus lenses are in use and camera shake is a problem.

How To Use Shutter Speed Priority

Load the film, select **S** on the aperture dial and the appropriate shutter speed on the shutter speed dial. If the red exposure indicator LED lights up in the viewfinder, this means that the camera has calculated a suitable aperture which it will set, when the release is activated. Should the minus LED light up, this means that the largest available aperture on the lens is insufficient for the existing lighting conditions. In this case you have to select a slower shutter speed, or use flash, or load a faster film. If the plus LED lights

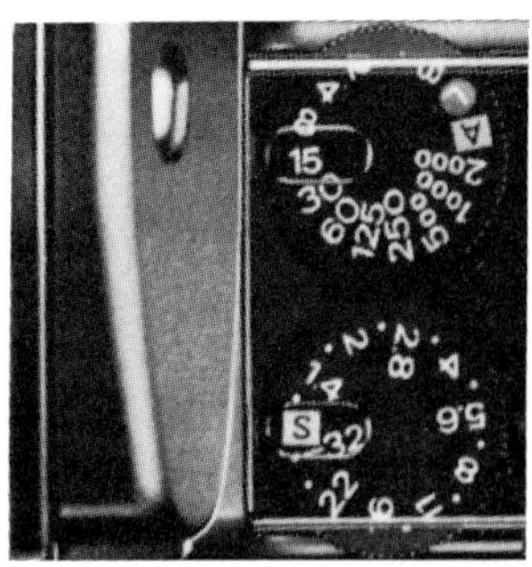

In shutter speed priority the aperture dial is set to **S** and a suitable speed between 1 and $^1/_{2000}$ sec. is chosen on the shutter speed dial. The viewfinder displays remain the same as in the program mode.

up, this means that the exposure control has calculated a of the selectable aperture value, i.e., that the smallest possible aperture opening is not small enough to avoid overexposure. In this case you will have to select a faster shutter speed, or use a neutral density filter, or load a slower film.

As you already know, the shutter of the F-401 cannot be released if the under- or overexposure warnings are lit up. If you wish to take the shot, despite these warnings – and this may be quite alright, as colour print films, in particular, can handle a certain amount of under- or overexposure, you have to change to manual exposure. In manual mode you must also not forget to select the aperture value on the aperture dial.

Shutter Speed Appropriate to the Subject

Fast-moving subjects and slow shutter speeds are, generally speaking, incompatible. A picture of a racing car, represented as a long red streak, will generally land in the wastepaper basket and not on a photographers' gallery wall. On the other hand, it is not always correct to totally freeze a movement on film. The petrified gymnast may be of some interest to the trainer, but most of us would not find such a representation very pleasing aesthetically. The art is to expose fast subjects in such a way that they are still acceptably sharp, but without depriving them of all movement. This obviously means choosing the right exposure time. If you have tried in the past and it did not turn out exactly to your liking, let me assure you that even experienced sports photographers produce over 90% of rubbish!

Still, you cannot rely entirely on good luck and happy coincidence. You could achieve your desired results by using up a lot of film, but it would be cheaper and less frustrating to bear a few helpful numbers in mind. It is possible to calculate in advance at what shutter speed a moving subject starts to become blurred. You will find a table below of popular subjects and blurring of movement. If you wish to show the moving subjects rather sharper, then you have to keep the

Movement Blur

Distance from the camera to the subject (with standard focal length)	**Direction of movement with respect to the film plane** ↕	✕	↔
Slow movement, pedestrian, children playing, cars up to 15mph			
4 m	1/125	1/250	1/500
8 m	1/60	1/125	1/250
16 m	1/30	1/60	1/125
Fast movement, running, fast sports, vehicles travelling faster than 30mph			
4 m	1/500	1/1000	1/2000 or with panning
8 m	1/250	1/500	1/1000
16 m	1/125	1/250	1/500
Very fast movement, vehicles travelling faster than 55 mph			
4 m	1/500	1/1000	1/2000 or with panning
8 m	1/250	1/500	1/1000
16 m	1/125	1/250	1/500

shutter speed a little faster than the suggested values. If you wish to make the movement more visible, then you need to expose for longer than the given times. You first estimate the speed of the subject, then set this speed on the camera.

By the way, movement of an object can be demonstrated very effectively to the viewer by showing it sharply against a blurred background. You achieve such results by panning in the direction of the movement. This too will take some practice and you will probably have to sacrifice a few films before you get the hang of it.

If you wish to represent movement by a certain amount of blurring, then the shutter speed priority mode is particularly well-suited for it. First you focus on a point which the subject will shortly cross. If this is difficult by autofocus then it will have to be done manually. Preselect the required shutter speed and check again in the viewfinder, whether the red LED indicates that the exposure setting is correct. Then you are ready to expose at the right moment.

Limits of Shutter Speed Priority

The shutter speed priority mode is always unsuitable when a precisely-defined depth of field is an important consideration. This applies to portraits, landscapes, architecture, and macro photography. In these cases aperture priority is the correct mode which allows you to open up for portraits, where a small depth of field is more flattering, or stop down to a small aperture to obtain maximum depth of field, as is desirable for landscape and macro photography.

Lenses that do not possess the electronic contacts which are present in Nikon AF lenses are just as unsuitable in shutter speed priority, as in any other exposure mode.

This is How Shutter Speed Priority Works

After the shutter speed had been selected and the release depressed the camera computer will signal that it has calculated an appropriate aperture value for the preselected shutter speed by lighting up the red exposure LED in the viewfinder. In the calculation of this aperture it assessed the subject brightness, the film speed, the preselected shutter speed and the aperture setting range, of the attached lens.

When the release is fully depressed the camera computer activates the diaphragm lever via an electromagnet and closes the aperture to the calculated value. Now the camera's electronics perform another measurement which takes some milliseconds. Based on this second measurement with working aperture the actual shutter speed is modified for absolutely correct exposure. This corrected shutter speed will be employed as soon as the mirror is raised and the exposure is made. This procedure ensures that any variations in the mechanical tolerances of the diaphragm are compensated for.

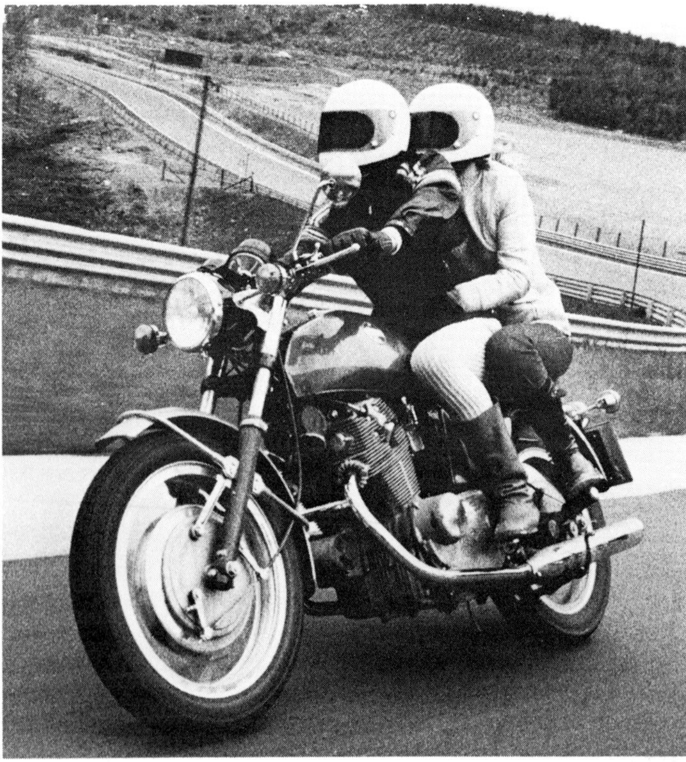

This is an enlargement from a shot taken with a 35mm lens from a distance of about 4m, with a shutter speed of $^1/_{1000}$ sec. Photo: Rudolf Dietrich

Creative Depth of Field with Aperture Priority Mode

In aperture priority mode the camera will choose a suitable shutter speed to go with the photographer's preselected aperture. Regardless of what focal length you are using, whether your subject is a landscape, a portrait, architecture or a macro shot, aperture priority is the ideal exposure mode for a wide range of subjects. However, in contrast to the program mode, the aperture priority mode requires a little skill from the photographer.

Using Aperture Priority Mode

Load the film, set the shutter speed dial to **A** and select the required aperture value on the aperture dial and you are ready to start. As long as the red exposure LED in the viewfinder remains lit, you are able to vary the aperture value to suit the particular subject. If the red exposure LED begins to blink, then this indicates that the preselected aperture is too small and that the automatically-calculated shutter speed may lead to camera shake.

If the minus LED lights up, this means that the calculated shutter speed for the preselected aperture exceeds one

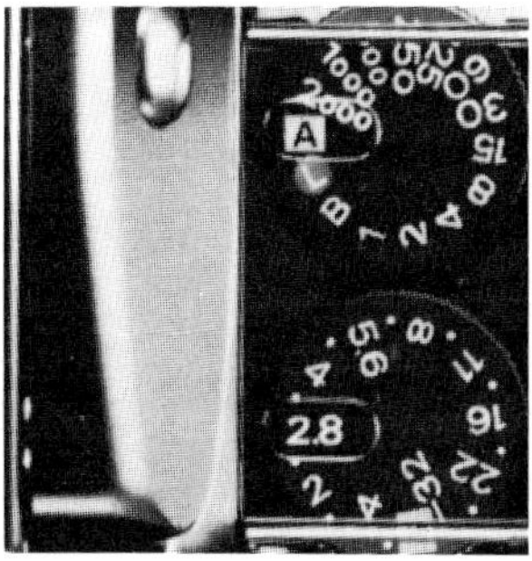

In the aperture priority mode the the shutter speed dial is set to **A** and a suitable aperture between f/1.4 and f/32 is selected. The viewfinder displays are mainly the same as for program mode.

second and can no longer be selected automatically. If opening up the aperture does not cure this, then you will have no other choice but to use a flash or to load a faster film.

If the plus LED is lit, this indicates a danger of overexposure. In this case you need to stop down or change to manual exposure.

Aperture Priority, Ideal for Portraits, Architecture and Landscapes

It makes no difference to the exposure level if you select aperture f/4 or f/16 in aperture priority mode. If your camera selects a shutter speed of $^1/_{1000}$ sec. for f/4, it will, under the same circumstances, select a shutter speed of $^1/_{60}$ sec. for f/16. The amount of light, and therefore the exposure level, will be the same in both cases. Apart from the relatively long exposure times which could result in camera-shake, any time/aperture combination producing an equivalent exposure level is as good as any other. This argument applies only to exposure level. Whether you want to produce a portrait against a sharp background or prefer a blurred background will determine whether the preselected aperture should be large or small. The decision of which aperture expresses your intentions best is yours.

The optimum aperture depends on the one hand on the subject, on the other, how you wish to treat it. Your ideas of how to present a scene can be totally subjective. If you wish to produce very sharp images, as for example in architectural photography, where every detail needs to be clearly reproduced, then you have to work with the aperture at which the lens produces its best results. Lens aberrations are an optical reality; they may be corrected but can never be removed completely. Theory says that, generally speaking, the performance of a lens is worst when the aperture is fully open because of spherical and chromatic aberrations, astigmatism, etc. Stopping down to the medium aperture values will produce the best reproduction results. If you stop down even further there will again be a decline in image quality due to increasing diffraction effects. Practical application and many lens tests have shown that optimal lens performance lies between f/5.6 and f/11. An aperture of f/8 or f/8-11 must therefore be considered the best advice if you are after fine details across the whole image. In the case of telephoto lenses smaller apertures may also be included.

Apart from definition, the aperture setting plays a major role in determining the depth of field. You may already know that it is impossible to represent a spatial subject uniformly sharp from a close distance to infinity. Only a few objects are two-dimensional, and most contain spatial elements, so only a certain range of their depth can be represented in sharp focus. Looking from the camera's viewpoint, the depth of field is from the least distance to the greatest distance between which the object is represented in acceptably sharp focus.

The human eye has no such problem. Therefore you should never rely on your own visual impressions when determining the depth of field of a shot. Focusing in the human eye is performed by the visual centre in the brain and is always adjusted to the area or point on which you are concentrating. As this is done without your being aware, you always have the impression that everything you see is always in perfect focus. When looking through your reflex camera, however, you are focusing on a certain point in the viewfinder and the depth of field comprises a limited range in front and behind your focusing point. How great this range is depends on the distance of your subject, on the aperture, and on the focal length of your lens.

Depth of Field Made to Measure

A general rule to remember is: long distance, small aperture and short focal length result in great depth of field. It will prove helpful if you can remember a few general values for your guidance. Using a lens with a focal length of 50mm at f/8, and focused on a subject 0.5m away, the depth of field will be 0.49m to 0.54m. If you focus on a subject at 3m, the depth of field will be from 2.2m to 5.2m. When focusing on a subject at 20m distance, the depth of field will stretch from 6m to infinity. If you focus the 50mm lens on infinity when using an aperture of f/8, the depth of field will extend from about 9m to infinity. These examples show clearly that the shorter the destance, the smaller the depth of field. In addition, you have to consider that it will extend further behind the focal point than in front of it. For medium focusing distances, and disregarding macro photography, the depth of field will extend twice as far beyond the focusing plane than towards the camera, or in other words: one-third in front and two-thirds behind the focusing plane.

Now if the focal length and focusing distance are fixed, the depth of field may be varied by changing the aperture. In the case of the 50mm lens, focusing on a subject at 3m distance from the camera with an aperture of f/1.2, the depth of field would be from 2.88m to 3.14m. If an aperture of f/5.6 is chosen, the depth of field is increased from 2.5m to 3.7m, and if the aperture is f/22, the depth of field is even greater, from 1.6m to 15m. As you can see, the depth of field increases with smaller apertures. For a distance setting of 5m the depth of field with an aperture of f/16 would be from 2.6m to 112m, and with an aperture of f/22 from 2m to infinity. You should make use of these facts. If your point of focus is determined by image frame and camera position, then you can determine the depth of field by choosing a larger or smaller aperture. If you take architectural shots where every detail is important, you will stop down to the smaller apertures, but in portrait photography, where a detailed background is only distracting, you would choose the large apertures to concentrate solely on the essentials.

The depth of field depends also on the focal length of the lens. The often-quoted rule that shorter focal lengths produce greater depth of field is only true if we assume a fixed camera position for the shot. Let's take, for example, a focusing distance of 4m and an aperture of f/8. With a 16mm lens, the depth of field will stretch from 0.8m to infinity. With a 28mm lens, it ranges from 1.8m to infinity, but if we take a 50mm lens, the range is reduced from 2.9m to 8m. As we have used the same camera location in our example, i.e. the same distance to the object, we find that with increasing focal length the reproduction scale becomes larger. This in turn means that the depth of field of a 16mm lens is considerably greater but the subject is represented as much smaller.

Now let us look at the other case where we photograph the same subject, using lenses with different focal lengths and with different camera positions, in such a way that for each focal length the subject is represented to the same reproduction ratio. Now you will have to move much closer to the subject with the wide-angle lens to obtain the same scale, than with a standard or even telephoto lens, and the depth of field in the wide-angle shot will shrink again, cancelling the original advantage. The rule of thumb of the gain in depth of field for the shorter focal lengths only applies therefore when we compare equal shooting distances. For equal reproduction ratios the gain in depth of field is more or less lost.

To summarize the different rules of depth of field for practical application:

- The greatest possible depth of field is obtained by exact focusing on the important feature in the subject and by stopping down the aperture to a small opening. If you are using the autofocus then the important subject detail should be kept within the autofocus metering field.
- If you wish to show only a certain part of your image in sharp focus, then you have to focus exactly on the required distance and select a relatively large aperture.

- If only the foreground up to the important feature is wanted in sharp focus, then you have to move the point of focus closer to the camera, and stop down just enough so that your important feature is only just in focus. This means you use the autofocus to focus on a subject detail closer to the camera, store the focus setting, realign the framing and then release.
- If the foreground needs to be somewhat out of focus and the important feature is in the background, then you have to relocate the point of focus, just beyond the required feature, and stop down as much as is necessary to bring it just into focus.

The depth of field diagrams or tables are an excellent aid if you are using the depth of field as the important aspect of your image creation. Such tables are supplied by Nikon with all their lenses and I have included them at the back of the book. You can read off the distance range within which a subject is in acceptably sharp focus for the various focal lengths. It is a good idea to browse through them to get a better idea of depth of field until you develop a feeling for this aspect of photography.

Available Light Photography with Aperture Priority

The F-401 is suitable for lengthy exposures in the aperture priority mode. The program modes are not suitable, as you have to take an active part in producing the shot in order to avoid the real danger of camera shake with long exposures. In any case you would be working within that range which enters the aperture priority mode, as you have to open the aperture wide under low lighting conditions. When using aperture priority mode you are still free to make your choice, even in dimly-lit conditions. Under certain circumstances, if you are taking stationary subjects, it could be advantageous to stop the aperture down again to increase depth of field.

I must mention here though that the long exposure range of the F-401 is somewhat limited as the slowest shutter speed setting is one second. Even so, this should not prevent you from undertaking this type of photography.

For lengthy exposures, whether at night in the open air, in a dark cathedral, or (if permitted) in a museum, I would recommend an ISO 400 daylight film. The ISO 640 artificial light film by Scotch may be suitable for situations lit solely by tungsten light. This film has been considerably improved in recent years and offers excellent quality for this speed. Personally I would use ISO 1000 or 1600 film only if this avoided the necessity to expose with shutter speeds slower than $^1/_{60}$ sec. These fast film speeds do have the advantage that one can use them without tripod. If the use of a tripod cannot be avoided then I usually choose an ISO 400 film. These are always better in quality with regard to sharpness, grain and colour rendering.

Whenever you are working with a tripod, or are supporting the camera in some other way, you should always use the self-timer for long exposures. This prevents camera shake when depressing the release. The electrical remote release is also suitable, of course, but don't forget the eyepiece cover! If your eye is not covering the eyepiece, light could enter from behind into the viewfinder and distort the exposure readings.

Long exposures would not be any problem if the reciprocity effect for daylight colour film did not make itself felt from about $^{1}/_{10}$ sec. In other words, the effective film speed declines with long exposure times. It may be necessary to overexpose by up to two stops to compensate, but this depends on the type and make of the film used, and on the level of exposure times.

Limits of Aperture Priority Mode

The aperture priority mode of the F-401 is unsuitable whenever a precisely-defined shutter speed is important for the subject in question. If the danger lies in camera shake, then the preselection of a suitable shutter speed is important, and you should choose shutter speed priority. If you take people at sport or play, you can capture your subjects quickly and creatively by preselecting a shutter speed that will either freeze the movement or allow its speed to be expressed by a precisely determined movement-blurred effect. As there is no information on shutter speed in the viewfinder in the aperture priority mode you should always switch to shutter speed priority.

As the F-401 depends on the electronic transfer of the smallest or largest available aperture opening of the lens used, you cannot use a whole range of lenses and accessories in the aperture priority mode, just as in all other program modes. All conventional adapters, bellows, slide duplicators and special lenses are unsuitable for the F-401. The only lenses that are suitable are the Nikon AF lenses with the characteristic electronic contacts. Moreover, changing over to manual exposure brings little joy to the user of an F-401. When in manual exposure mode, only the under- and overexposure warnings will indicate whether your chosen settings are correct, and this only with Nikon AF lenses. If you use any other lens then the entire exposure metering system will not work and you must use a hand-held exposure meter.

This is How Aperture Priority Works

After you have selected a suitable aperture on the aperture dial and the metering system has been activated by depressing the release to first pressure position, the camera computer will calculate the appropriate shutter speed. Completion of this sequence can be seen when the red exposure LED lights up in the viewfinder. The F-401 uses open aperture metering and the exposure value is therefore calculated from the electronically transmitted value set on the aperture dial. This is possible only if the electronic lens contacts are capable of transmitting their smallest and largest available aperture openings. The aperture will be stopped down to the selected value only after the release is fully depressed. The exposure control then makes another measurement and adjusts the shutter speed for the preselected aperture to produce the correct exposure level. Now the mirror is raised and the shutter blinds opened. Any inaccuracies in the aperture therefore have no effect on the exposure. This trick of re-measuring at the last moment is employed not only in aperture priority mode, but also in program mode. It is also the reason why the exposure control of the F-401 is so exact.

Automatic Exposure Correction by Triple Sensor Light Metering

There are many shooting situations where the automatic exposure control of most cameras is unreliable. The exposure corrections required in special situations require some expertise and forward-thinking by the photographer. The Image Master Control System of the F-401 carries out such exposure corrections based on the metering results from its triple sensor light metering system.

I must admit, I was rather sceptical to start with. How correctly would this triple sensor metering assess the situation and how well would the camera computer process this information? One cannot say that Nikon is a newcomer in the field of camera technology; after all, the FA already incorporated a five-sensor metering system, which worked perfectly in a variety of situations. Even so, there were failures. This is not surprising – to obtain perfect results with multiple sensor readings, one would need nine metering points, and the processing of this information would need its own computer. This is the requirement if the camera is supposed to perform automatic exposure corrections in all situations.

Now the F-401 is supposed to perform this job better or just as well with only three sensors. I have put several films through the F-401, assessing its performance in a variety of extreme situations and I arrived at a very favourable conclusion. Admittedly, there are situations where the F-401 is no better than any other SLR camera with conventional centre-weighted integral metering. On the other hand, in a variety of situations the F-401 produced noticeably better exposed pictures and I found only one instance where the F-401, with the triple sensor metering, produced a worse result than a camera with centre-weighted metering would

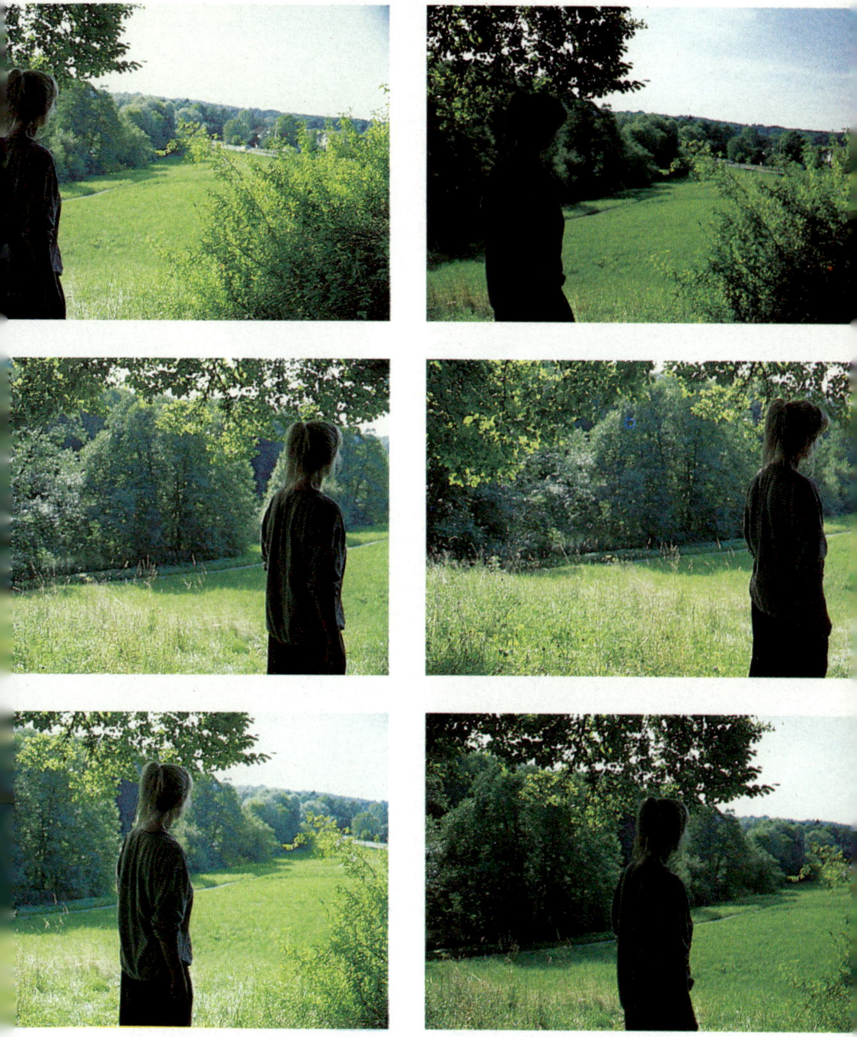

This is how well the triple sensor metering works. The pictures on the left were taken by triple sensor metering. Despite the contrast the camera has managed to compensate and show the main subject properly exposed. With conventional integral metering in the pictures on the right, this proved to be much more uncertain. *Photo: Michael Huber*

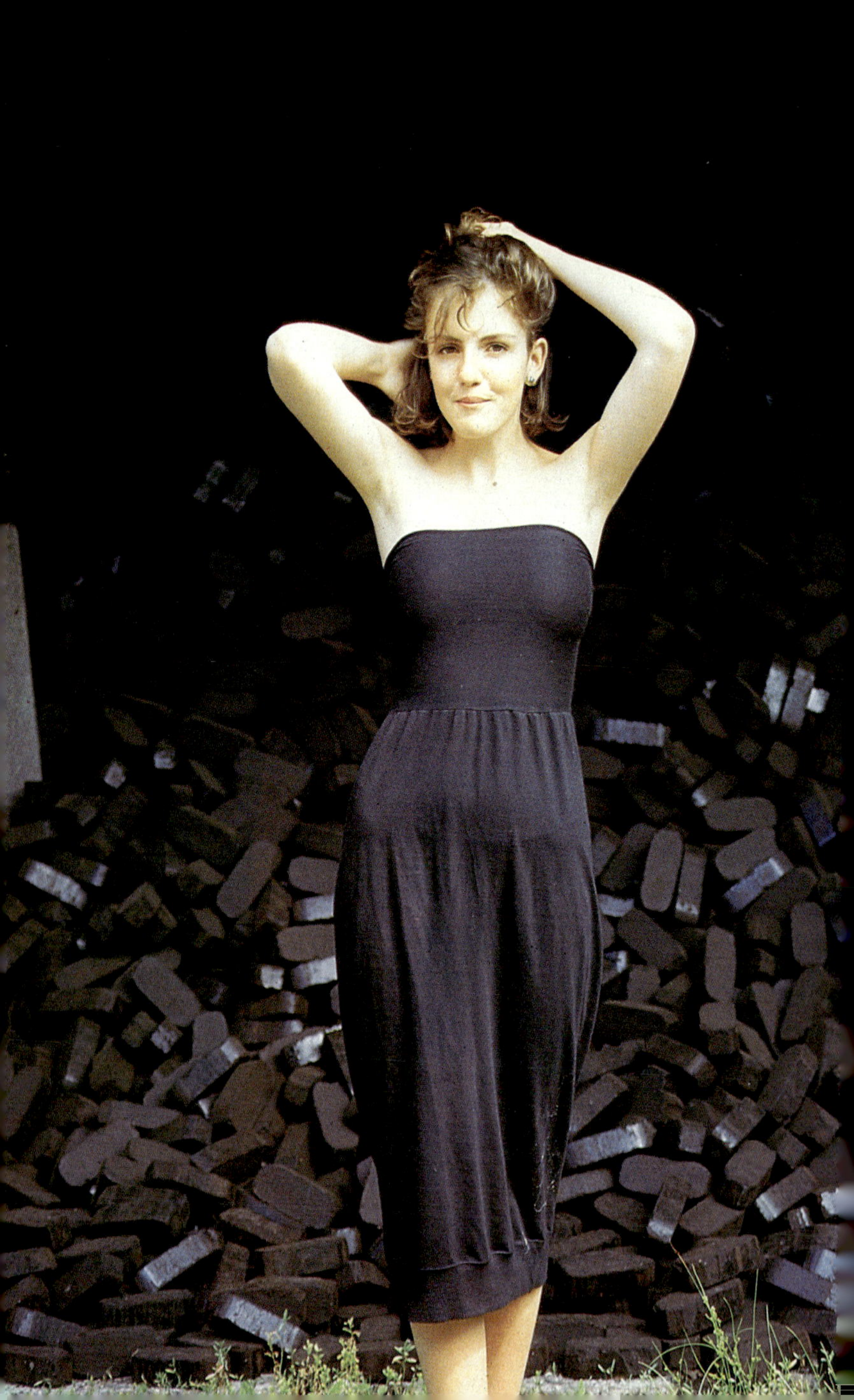

have done. My conclusion therefore is a definite yes to this new development by Nikon.

Using the Automatic Exposure Correction

The F-401 will use automatic exposure correction in all automatic exposure modes, regardless of whether you are in program, shutter speed or aperture priority mode. You need not perform any special settings or worry about anything!

Limits of Triple Field Light Metering

The Image Master Control's assessment of whether the subject presented to the F-401 is light or dark obviously depends on the film speed. This could cause an incorrect exposure for some types of subject. Certain extreme subjects, such as "black-on-black" or an averagely bright subject in front of an extremely dark background, or the "white-on-white" subject in rather dim lighting, will not be exposed to the best possible effect with the F-401 (but better than with centre-weighted integral metering). If you are faced with such a situation and you wish to improve on the automatic facilities, then you have to de-activate the triple-sensor metering by releasing the AEL button and change to manual exposure control.

In situations such as this you should not rely on the triple sensor metering of the F-401. Subjects consisting of black on black would be shown unnaturally light. It is best to use manual exposure control by metering the face across the full frame and then recompose to take the picture. *Photo: Michael Huber*

Changing to Centre-Weighted Metering by AEL Button

Should you wish to de-activate the triple sensor metering in the aperture priority and shutter speed priority exposure modes, then you will have to depress the AEL button while the viewfinder diplay is activated. This de-activates the triple-sensor metering and activates centre-weighted metering. As long as you keep the AEL button depressed, the centre-weighted metering value of the subject last

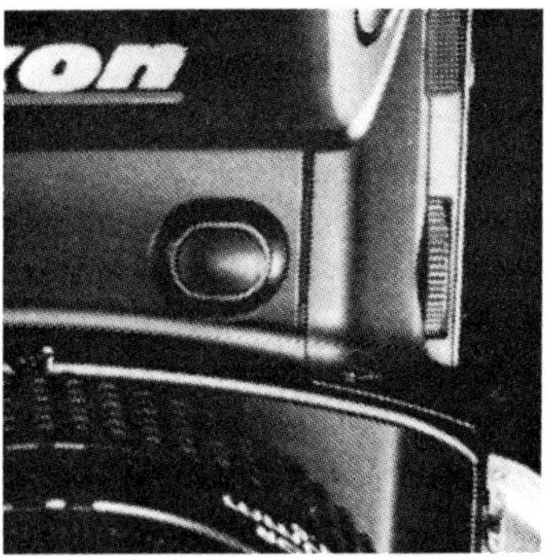

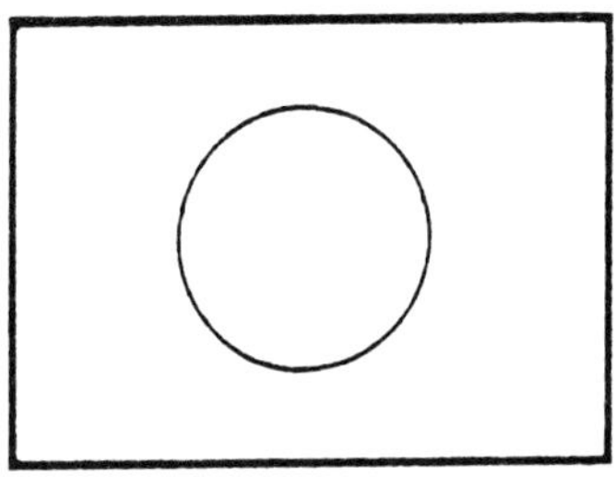

When the AEL button is depressed the camera changes to centre-weighted metering. As long as the button is kept depressed, the last metered value is stored. The 12mm metering circle serves to measure the subject.

measured, stays in memory. If you now depress the release, the exposure will be made with this metering value. Merely depressing the AEL button will not bring about an improved exposure; you have to ensure that the main subject lies within the 12mm metering circle at the centre of the viewfinder and fills this area as fully as possible. The sequence of actions is therefore as follows: point at the main subject, depress the AEL button, keep the AEL button depressed, re-align the camera for the required framing and depress the release fully to take the shot.

This is How the Automatic Exposure Correction Works

Correct exposure with conventional metering is impossible for many subjects, because the contrasts contained within the subject are too great and the film cannot cope with such a wide range. Expressed another way: the difference between the brightest and the darkest parts of the subject are too great, and the photographer has to decide which is the more important, the darker or the lighter portions. If the photographer does not make a decision, the camera will produce pictures that are either too light or too dark. One well-known example is the backlit portrait. With conventional centre-weighted integral metering the very bright background would cause the face to be underexposed, the result: a silhouette. To obtain a correctly-exposed portrait with this type of metering system, the main subject would have to fill the frame almost completely to allow the camera to obtain the correct readings. This is also possible with the F-401 and is described in the chapters on manual exposure.

Luckily you need not worry, because the F-401 performs such corrections automatically. Automatic or not, it is interesting to know how this is achieved and to know if one can, and should, rely on the exposure corrections of the F-401.

The lens projects the image onto a mirror and from there into the pentaprism from where it is projected in a secondary beam onto a triple sensor. The triple sensor consists of three metering areas. The central metering area corresponds more or less to the single sensor of a centre-weighted integral meter. The additional metering areas to the right and left, cover the remaining areas to the right and left of the central circle. The signals from these peripheral areas however, are not assigned the same weighting as the central area, but are strongly attenuated.

The Image Master Control of the F-401 assesses the

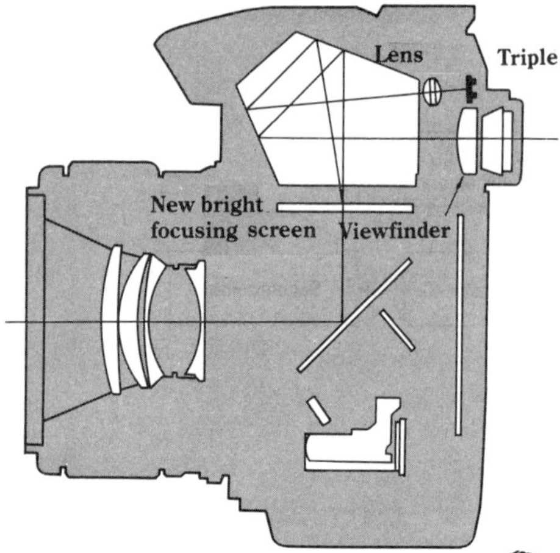

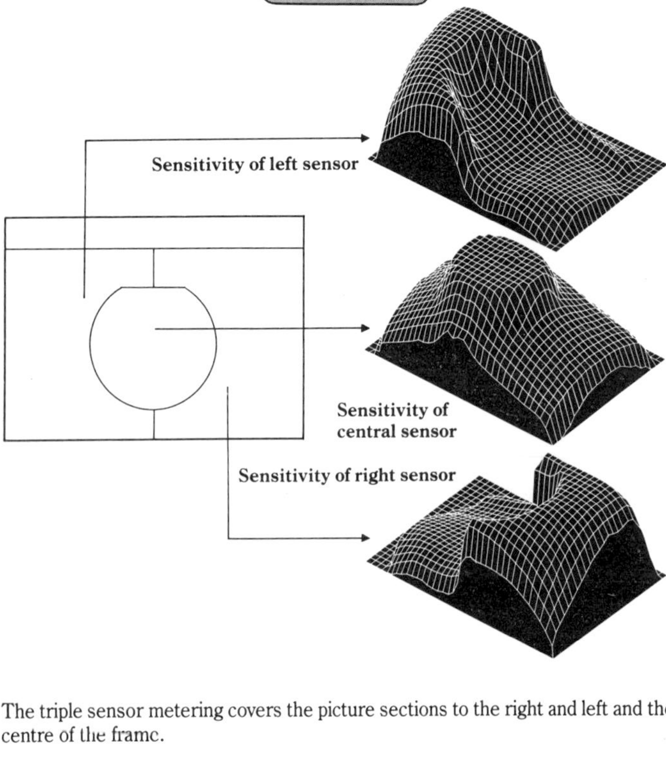

The triple sensor metering covers the picture sections to the right and left and the centre of the frame.

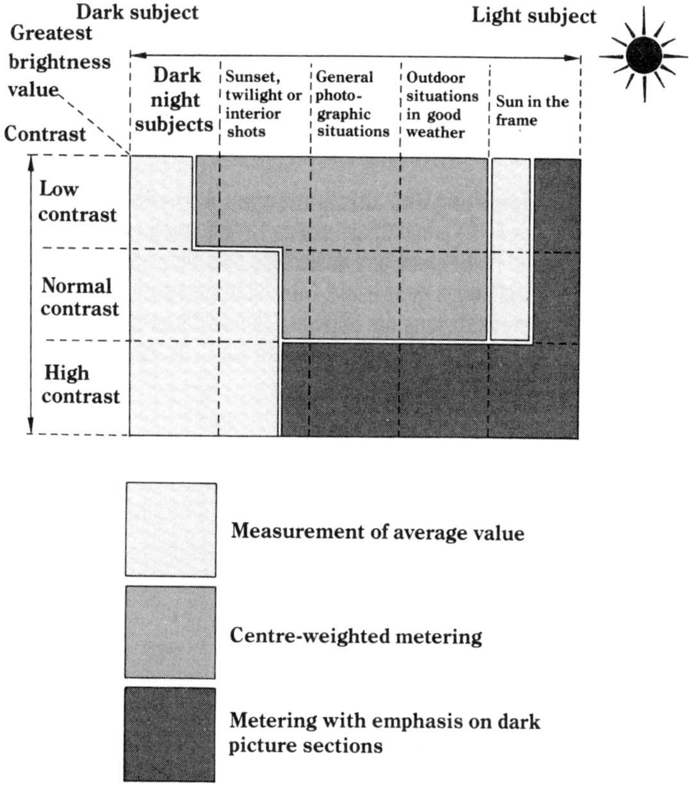

The camera computer evaluates the subject according to its general brightness and contrast. According to this result it will either expose for the average, for centre-weighted or for the dark parts.

metering results of the three areas as follows:

○ It assesses the average brightness across the three metering areas, disregarding extremely light and extremely dark areas.
○ It remembers the value of the darkest metering field.
○ It remembers the value for the centre field, which corresponds to the area for the conventional centre weighted metering.

- ○ It determines the differences in brightness – the contrast between the brightest and the darkest field.

Based on this assessment the Image Master Control System is capable of recognising typical subjects, with a great degree of certainty, and adjusting the exposure accordingly.

Very dimly-lit subjects. For example: night shots in the open, or situations indoors in dimly-lit rooms.

In such situations a few brighter light sources, possible light points in an otherwise very dark area, are quite typical. This means that the average brightness is very low, but the contrast could be quite high. If the exposure is based on centre-weighted metering the result would be either much too dark, because the central area may accidentally contain some bright light source, or too light, because the system tries to overexpose as the metering area contained only dark areas. The Image Master Control, on the other hand, will produce a reasonably exposed picture, as it assesses the average value across the three metering areas.

Subjects with very little brightness. For example: a sunset, dusk or reasonably well-lit interiors.

If the contrast is low, then the F-401 will automatically expose according to a centre-weighted assessment, and the main subject that is generally positioned at the centre of the frame will be particularly well exposed. On the other hand, if the contrast is high, then the F-401 will automatically expose for the average value to avoid accidental exposure for a single light source in a dark corner. The F-401 is therefore quite capable of coping with subjects of this type.

Normally bright to above-average bright subjects. For example: typical situations outdoors in bright daylight and in average weather:

In average contrast conditions the F-401 exposes in a centre-weighted fashion and generally "captures" the main subjects particularly well. If the contrast is rather high, then the F-401 assumes a backlit condition and exposes for the dark subject areas. In most situations this assessment is correct and the resulting pictures are exactly right.

Very bright subjects. For example: situations where the sun itself is in the frame, or perhaps very bright sunshine with reflecting areas such as the sea:

For average or low contrasts the F-401 will expose for centre-weighted values across the three metering areas. Subjects where the contrast is low or average are generally uniformly illuminated and the resulting picture has a natural effect. If the contrast is high, on the other hand, then the Image Master Control will assess this as a backlit subject, where the dark areas need to be overexposed for correct rendering. Using a conventional camera one would have to bring the important subject detail completely into the central metering area or to make exposure corrections to produce equally good results.

Extremely bright subjects. For example: a white sandy beach or a field covered in snow, bathed in bright sunlight, or a view of the sun itself:

In situations such as these the F-401 will automatically overexpose. This means you will automatically get the corrections necessary for backlit shots. If the subject is not only very light in colour, but also extremely well-lit, then the natural tonal values are usually very well reproduced.

Manual Exposure

In the manual shooting mode you are able to expose very precisely, provided you are capable of assessing the metering results, and have chosen the correct subject detail to be metered. Assessment of metering results in manual mode is not taken care of by the camera computer. Therefore, as well as being familiar with the metering characteristics of your camera, you also have to know what exposure correction you have to apply for a given situation. If you are capable of correct manual exposure you can achieve even better results than the automatic exposure corrections performed by the F-401. I need to mention though that manual exposure is rather cumbersome with the F-401 and takes a little time. For this reason I would recommend it only if it is absolutely necessary.

This is How You Use Manual Exposure

Whenever the shutter speed dial is set to a time between $^1/_{2000}$ and 1 sec., and the aperture dial is set to a value between f/1.4 to f/22, then the F-401 functions in manual exposure. The display in the viewfinder will be a plus or a minus sign, as long as the chosen aperture/shutter speed combination is incorrect for the subject. As soon as the metered results are adjusted, the red exposure LED will light up.

To adjust the setting you therefore have to point at the main subject and adjust the aperture and shutter speed until the red exposure LED is lit. Let's assume the shutter speed dial is set to $^1/_{125}$ sec. and the aperture to f/8 and the plus LED lights up in the viewfinder. You now have the choice of either leaving the aperture at f/8 and increasing the shutter speed, to perhaps $^1/_{500}$ sec. Or you can leave the shutter speed at

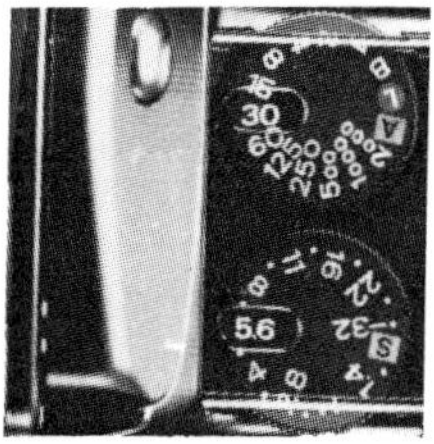

Correct manual exposure setting (+/– $^{1}/_{3}$ EV)	**○ on**
Manual: + 1 EV to + $^{1}/_{3}$ EV	**+○ on**
Manual: – $^{1}/_{3}$ EV to – 1EV	**–○ on**
Manual: more than 1EV brighter	**+ on**
Manual: more than 1EV darker	**– on**

Shutter speed and aperture are set on the shutter speed and aperture dials of the camera. The display in the viewfinder will indicate whether the exposure is correct.

the original value and adjust the aperture to a higher number, i.e. f/11 or f/16, etc. In any case, you have to alter either the shutter speed, or the aperture or a combination of both, to reduce the original exposure setting until the red exposure LED lights up, together with the plus LED. Now you know that you are within one stop of the correct exposure level. After stopping down one more stop or reducing the shutter speed to the next shortest time, only the exposure LED should remain lit. If the minus LED lights up instead, then you know you must increase by half a stop to stay at the correct exposure level.

As soon as the correct exposure level has been achieved you are quite free to change the aperture/shutter speed combination to suit the given situation. However, don't forget to open up the aperture whenever you increase the shutter speed, and *vice versa*, stopping down for slower shutter speeds. If the viewfinder display indicates that correct exposure level is obtained at, say, f/11 and $^{1}/_{250}$ sec., then you can also use f/16 and $^{1}/_{125}$ sec., or f/8 and $^{1}/_{500}$ sec.

When metering the subject you can use the 12mm circle at the centre of the viewfinder as an aid. In the manual exposure mode the F-401 uses centre-weighted metering, i.e. the area within the 12mm metering circle accounts for 60% of the metering result. For very contrasty subjects such as, for example, backlit subjects, this centre-weighted metering is not quite sufficient to produce the correct result. In such a situation you will have to move closer to the subject so that it fills the entire viewfinder. Now you can take the reading, which you store manually. You can then move away to the required distance, adjust the framing for the required view, and take the shots.

Individual Exposure with Manual Setting

How should you take your light reading and what correction factors should you apply? Metering the subject for its average grey, that is average brightness, would be the simplest. Whether the subject is uniformly bright or very contrasty does not matter as long as you find the average point. You simply aim your camera at that point and set the time and aperture to the combination that will result in the red exposure LED lighting up in the viewfinder to indicate the correct exposure level. Thereafter you can choose the framing that suits you as the exposure is already stored. If you wish to show this average point a little darker or lighter, then you can make the appropriate correction. In many cases it is quite impossible to locate such an average grey value, so what should you do then? Also you may not be sure what subject point corresponds to what brightness. Good advice such as "meter those areas of light or shade where there are still clearly discernible contrasts" is often less than helpful. There is, however, one very good metering point to be found on one of the commonest subjects – the face. In summer, for beach photos, the tonal quality of the average European complexion corresponds closely to the average grey. Therefore if you are taking a picture against the sun you can meter the face across the entire viewfinder and then re-compose your picture and you will be more often right than wrong. A very pale complexion, which is also supposed to appear pale in the picture, has to be taken with an exposure correction of $+2/3$ stop. A dark complexion needs an exposure correction of up to $-2/3$ stop to give a natural representation.

In many cases the use of a grey card, generally available from a dealer, would be very useful. You put this card, which has a reflectance of 18%, within the subject field and you then have the ideal metering area. However, it could be that your subject is not lit very uniformly, parts lying in very dark shade whilst the rest might be in direct sunlight. Under such circumstances you have to place the grey card within that section of your subject which contains the important detail. If you want to represent average grey a little lighter or a little darker, then you will have to make the appropriate corrections.

If your main subject is black, and you do not want it to be represented as an average grey, then you will be best advised to use manual mode and not rely on the exposure evaluation of the Image Master Control. You simply meter the black area and use the resulting value with a correction of −2 stops, the black will then be shown black in your picture. To make this correction you adjust the exposure until the exposure LED lights up, then increase the shutter speed (shorter time) or reduce the aperture (higher number) by two stops. In the same way you will have to make corrections for objects which are mainly white in your photograph. As a rule in this case you can use a correction factor of up to +2 stops.

As mentioned previously, the manual exposure setting on the F-401 should be used only if you are sure you will achieve a better result than the electronic control. Don't fiddle around with it unnecessarily, after all, why should you try and work it all out manually, when you have a perfectly good electronic metering and evaluation system at your fingertips that can do it quicker and better than you? Only when you are presented with problematic subjects, when you have to meter a precisely-defined area of subject across the whole viewfinder, be it a face, or a grey card, be it a predominantly black or white subject, will the manual method, together with exposure corrections, definitely produce the better results.

Manual Exposure is Ideal for Complicated Subjects

If you are watching a football match and use the procedure: point camera, meter, apply possible exposure correction, focus, release – you are definitely too slow. In such cases the automatic exposure control of the Image Master Control would definitely be faster and more reliable. But you won't believe me when I say that, as cumbersome as the manual setting might appear to be, sometimes it can be the best method for fast shots. There are moving subjects which are not particularly suitable for automatic exposure. Just think about footballers in white shorts on a green field. Depending on how much white is concentrated in the framing you have chosen, or in the centre metering zone, you will have under- or overexposure, or perhaps you were lucky and the exposure turned out right. For this reason professional photographers always use a preset exposure setting for difficult subjects which are not easy to handle in the automatic mode. To do this you first measure the face of one of the footballers as close-up as possible. The values you obtain in this way for the aperture and shutter speed should be correct for the whole game, unless, of course, the lighting conditions change.

Extremely Fast with Manual Presetting

The statement that shooting with autofocus is particularly fast, strictly speaking, is only correct if the main subject is at the centre of the viewfinder, i.e. within the AF metering field. If this is not the case then you have to first meter the main subject and store the focusing result. Only then can you re-align the camera for the required framing and release. With a little practice this whole process should be quite fast.

Another difficult, if not impossible, situation is when the subject moves so fast across the frame that the AF focusing system has no chance to focus on it. This is also the reason why professional photographers, who have to earn their living in sports photography, smile condescendingly at this new-fangled facility. They use a different method: prefocus on a distance where the subject is expected to cross. Set an aperture/shutter speed combination that provides a sufficient depth of field and at the same time a short enough shutter speed to capture the subject. Then you only need to depress the release when an interesting scene presents itself.

With this method the shot can be taken as quickly as it takes you to decide when to press the release.

This trick is quite easily applied with the F-401. You will need to use an AF lens of the appropriate focal length, e.g. the AF 70-210mm,f/4.0 Zoom and perhaps an ISO 400 or even an ISO 1000 film.

Set the camera to manual exposure mode **M** and choose a suitable aperture and shutter speed. Now turn the manual focusing ring on the lens to focus on a distance where you expect the event to take place that you want to photograph. Now you are ready to release the shutter at any time. If the event takes place at the anticipated location, you can release immediately and the pictures will almost always be in sharp focus. As you have used a faster film, you should be able to use a small enough aperture to give you sufficient depth of field.

In addition, you could allow the focus-assist facility of the F-401 to provide the extra help in the decision when to release the shutter. Look through the viewfinder and, if the event takes place in the centre of the viewfinder, the green in-focus LED will light up to indicate that it is in sharp focus. If you release now you can be absolutely sure that the picture will be sharp.

As you can see, manual presetting in combination with the AF focus-assist facility is the fastest method. In automatic focusing the focusing metering and indication is exceedingly fast. What takes the time is the motorized focusing of the lens. You need not wait for this with the method described, but allow the moving subject to come into focus, at which point you release the shutter.

Manual Exposure Assumes Photographic Expertise

The correct measurement of the subject and the appropriate setting of aperture and shutter speed is the basis of every correctly-exposed picture, regardless of whether it is done electronically or manually. In the automatic modes the photographer need not take much notice of the technical aspects and I have kept my explanations in this respect to the necessary minimum. If we consider manual exposure, then the level of expertise has to be much higher. Now it is not just an advantage, but a necessity, to know the inter-relationships between exposure, subject brightness, exposure metering, film speed, aperture and shutter speed.

Exposure Metering

Only if the camera's electronics know exactly how bright a subject is, will the automatic exposure mode be capable of providing correct exposure. Even if you wish to set the exposure manually, you first have to meter the subject. Therefore the correct sequence is always: measure the subject, then decide on the correct exposure. But metering is not just metering! Depending on whether you meter the whole subject equally, or assign more importance to the central area, or meter only certain subject areas, we are talking of integral metering, centre-weighted integral metering or spot metering. The metering system of the F-401, as it is employed in manual mode and also when the

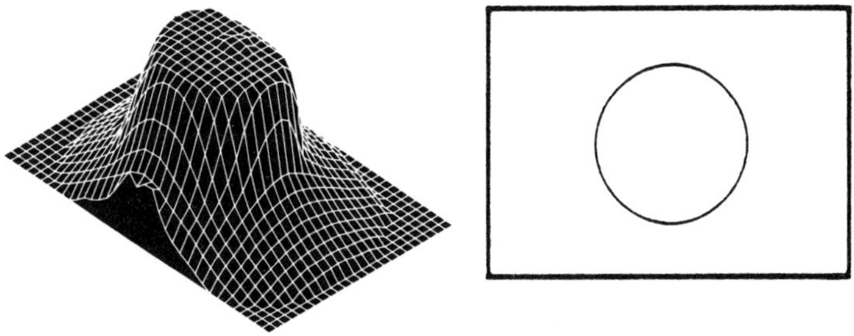

In manual exposure control the 12mm circle at the centre will contribute 60% of the subject brightness to the exposure reading (centre-weighted metering)

AEL button is activated, may be most aptly described as strongly centre-weighted integral metering. The central 13% of the picture area is assigned about 60% of the overall metering result, the remaining 87% of the picture area contributes only 40% towards the metering result. The contributions towards the metering results decline towards the edges, so the areas on the immediate edges contribute practically nothing. In most cases this is very reasonable, because we usually place unimportant details such as a bright sky at the edge, and if this were metered it would distort the overall metering result. On the other hand, the details placed at the centre of the picture are usually the most important which need to be correctly exposed.

If you are taking a person against a bright sky, then it could easily happen that the latter leads the exposure control to assume that the overall subject is rather bright so that the brightness of the person, the main subject, is not properly considerd and the result will be an underexposed picture. If the person is exactly at the centre of the picture when the subject is metered, then it could happen that they are correctly exposed first time. For this reason I have recommended that the main subject should always be brought into the centre of the viewfinder so that it completely covers the central metering area. The 12mm circle outlined at the centre of the viewfinder is very handy for this purpose as it defines reasonably well the outline of the 60%

centre-weighted metering area.

Then there is the question as to how the exposure meter is calibrated. All meters are calibrated so that an average grey subject is represented as the same average grey. This "average grey" in photography corresponds to a subject of average brightness, or more precisely, a subject with an average reflectivity of 18%. A subject which is defined as average grey therefore reflects 18% of incident light. So if we photograph a piece of card having a reflectivity of 18% (like the Kodak grey card) across the whole frame, then the exposure measurement system in the camera will measure the reflected light, compare this level of brightness with its internal calibrated standard, and calculate the correct exposure taking into account the set film speed.

It is unimportant in principle whether the exposure time is calculated for the preset aperture (aperture priority); whether the aperture is calculated for a preset shutter speed (shutter speed priority); whether an automatically set shutter speed and aperture combination is used (program mode); or whether a manually selected aperture and shutter speed combination is chosen.

If the camera works properly, then it is this exposure value that will reproduce the grey card correctly as a colour print with normal enlargement or as a colour slide when viewed at the correct brightness. You can check this by comparing a colour print with the original grey card. Of course, development of the film must be properly carried out and the correct exposure must be given when printing from the negative. To compare a slide with the grey card is a little more difficult. After all, the reproduction of the slide also depends on the brightness of the projection light. In any case, provided the exposure and processing of the slide film was correct, the

---

Two pictures of boats, in both used as an essential part of the composition. In the top view the wide-angle view of the boats emphasised in the foreground points to the fact that this is a fishing village. The beach scene of the boats taken from above with a telephoto lens lend them a very special character.
Photo: Wolf Huber

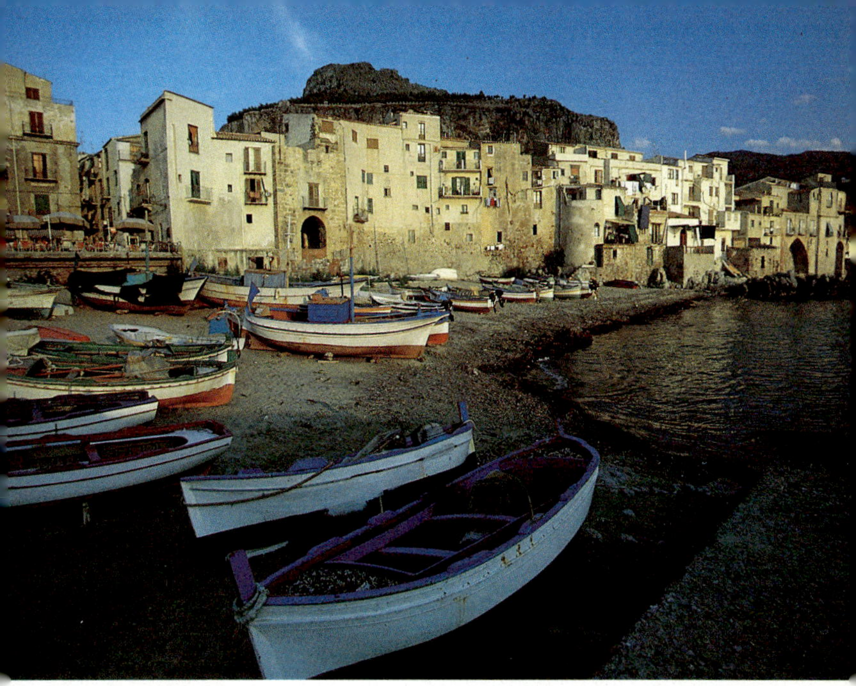

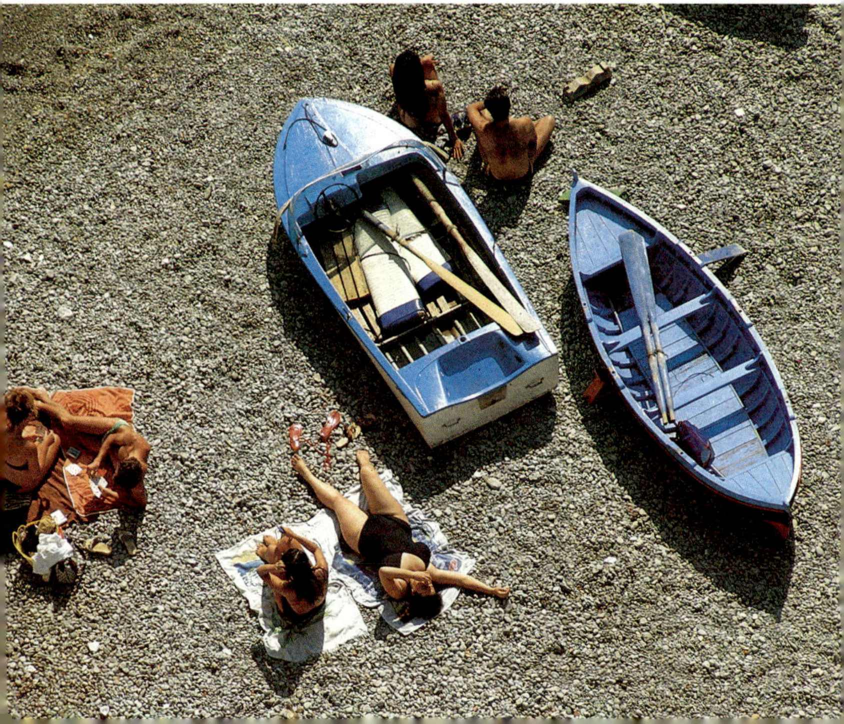

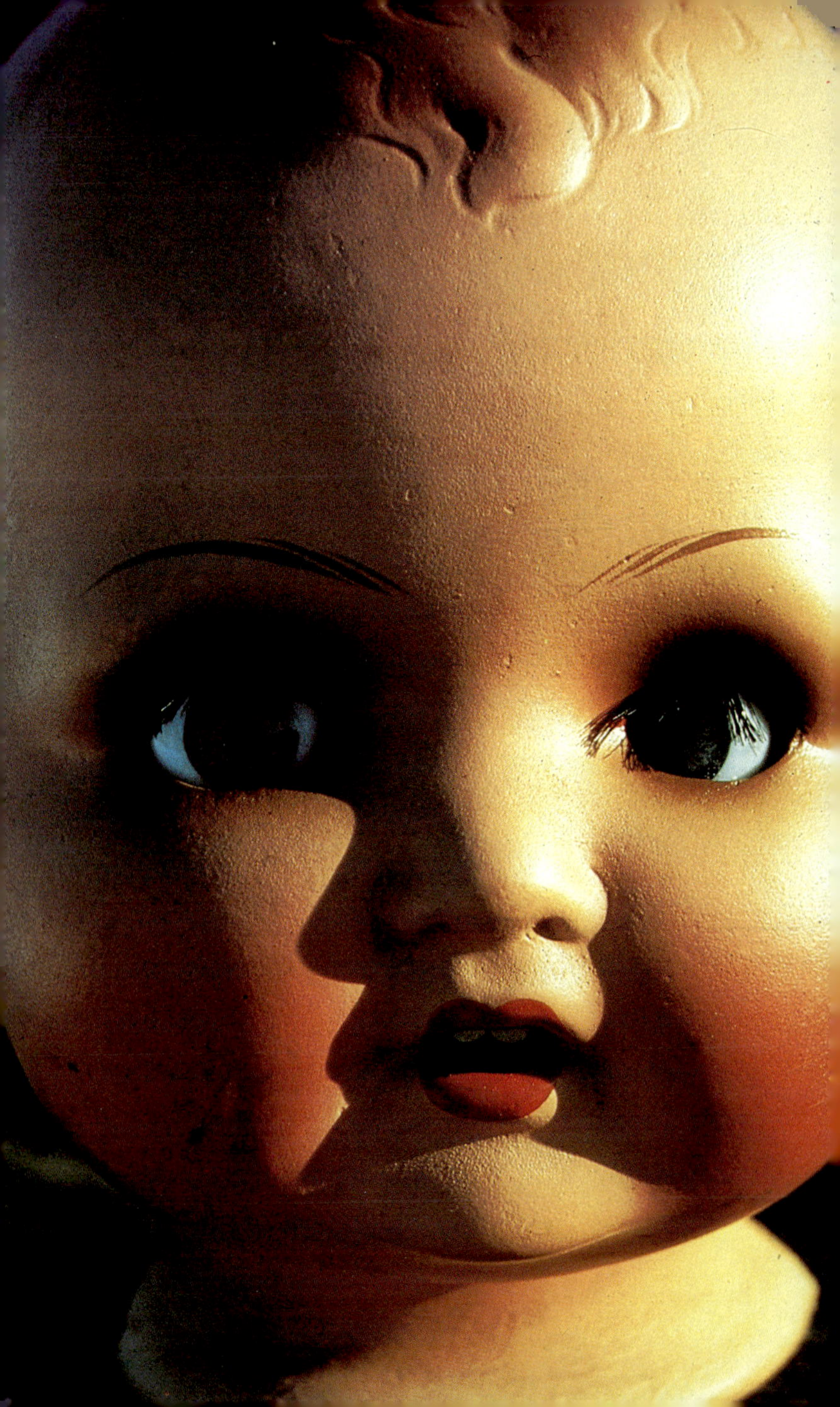

colour reproduction of the projected slide must give the impression that the brightness lies roughly halfway between black and white.

Whether an average uniformly average grey object is lit by a bright light or by a dim light does not matter, the camera has to adjust the exposure so that an actual average grey is always reproduced as such. Unfortunately most subjects are not uniform in brightness. Just think about the example of the back-lit shot. If you take a group of people against a bright sky, then the bright light from the unimportant background will dominate the light measurement and result in a relatively high average brightness for the overall picture. The exposure level calculated by the camera will result in the group of people being represented as silhouettes against the light. To compensate for this incorrect measurement, due to the high contrast, you will have to increase the exposure level by up to two stops. This means that the necessary exposure correction will depend on how much sky is included in the frame and where the bright sky lies with respect to the centre-weighted measuring circle of the F-401. Only after this compensation has been applied will the important statements in the picture be correctly represented, i.e. correct in their tone rendition. The blue in the sky will probably no longer be apparent and any white clouds will have merged into the washed-out sky. When using the F-401 in one of the automatic modes, you need not worry about exposure corrections for contrasty subjects, the triple sensor metering and Image Master Control will take care of this automatically.

Apart from very contrasty subjects, with a wide brightness range and where the dark and bright areas are unbalanced, there are other subjects with problematic reflectivity. One is

---

To collect antiques without incurring the expenditure, keep a photograph! This doll's head was picked up at a flea market with a medium telephoto lens.
Photo: Wolf Huber

where white is on white, and the other is where black is on black. If you photograph a snow-covered landscape you will usually be disappointed: the brilliant white snow turns out to be a dirty grey. The camera's light metering system has interpreted it as an average grey subject, but extremely well-lit, and indicated a very small exposure to compensate. If the snow needs to stay white, it will be necessary to compensate by up to two stops. Only if you are using a fast film and the brightness level is very high, will the Image Master Control of the F-401 assign an exposure correction in the automatic exposure modes. With normal lighting and average to slow films, you would be better advised to use manual exposure and apply the appropriate exposure correction. At the other extreme the camera will interpret a dark cellar as badly-lit average grey and it will be necessary to underexpose by up to two stops to achieve a good black. This situation is beyond the capabilities of the Image Master Control and you will always have to choose manual exposure to get it right.

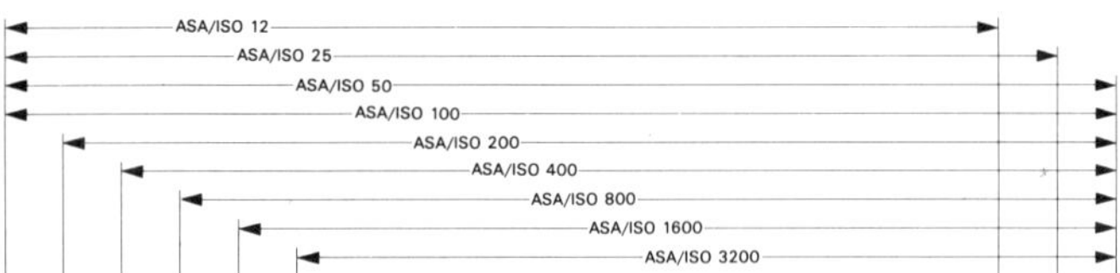

f/ \ EV	1	2	3	4	5	6	7	8	9	10	11	12	13	14	15	16	17	18	19
1,4	1	1/2	1/4	1/8	1/15	1/30	1/60	1/125	1/250	1/500	1/1000	1/2000							
2		1	1/2	1/4	1/8	1/15	1/30	1/60	1/125	1/250	1/500	1/1000	1/2000						
2,8			1	1/2	1/4	1/8	1/15	1/30	1/60	1/125	1/250	1/500	1/1000	1/2000					
4				1	1/2	1/4	1/8	1/15	1/30	1/60	1/125	1/250	1/500	1/1000	1/2000				
5,6					1	1/2	1/4	1/8	1/15	1/30	1/60	1/125	1/250	1/500	1/1000	1/2000			
8						1	1/2	1/4	1/8	1/15	1/30	1/60	1/125	1/250	1/500	1/1000	1/2000		
11							1	1/2	1/4	1/8	1/15	1/30	1/60	1/125	1/250	1/500	1/1000	1/2000	
16								1	1/2	1/4	1/8	1/15	1/30	1/60	1/125	1/250	1/500	1/1000	1/2000

Shutter speed

The lower limit of the metering range is shifted towards the higher EVs with increasing film speed.

The Metering Range Depends on the Film Speed

The F-401 sets the film speed automatically by DX coding from ISO 25 to ISO 5000. The practice of camera manufacturers is to use the ISO speeds. These are used throughout this book. It means that if a film speed was formerly described as 100 ASA, it now ISO 100. Stated in full, this is 100/21°, the log speed being used with some exceptional cameras and meters.

The film speed set by the camera affects the control and measuring range of the camera's electronics. For an ISO 100 film this ranges officially from EV1 (corresponding to aperture f/1.4 and 1 sec.) to EV19 (aperture f/16 and $^{1}/_{2000}$ sec.). Unofficially the control range extends even to EV21 (f/32 with $^{1}/_{2000}$ sec.), provided the lens used offers this aperture value. If a fast film is used, then the metering and control range is restricted in the lower range. This means, for example, that for an ISO 3200 film the longest exposure would be $^{1}/_{30}$ sec. at f/1.4 (corresponding to EV6).

Aperture and Exposure Time

How is a correctly exposed picture created? We start with the brightness of the subject, and this in turn is partly dependent on the intensity of the illuminating light source. If we think of outdoor photography we will appreciate that it makes a difference if the subject is in bright sunshine, if it is spring, summer, autumn or winter, what time of day it is, and whether or not it is cloudy. Artificial light sources too are of varying intensity; there is a considerable difference between an ordinary tungsten lamp and a photographic halogen lamp.

The light falling on the subject is reflected. The part that you can observe through the viewfinder is exactly the same as that which exposes the film. The brightness of the image projected onto the film plane depends on how much light is allowed to pass through the lens. This in turn is adjustable by a variable-sized opening in the lens – the so-called iris diaphragm which controls the aperture. Practically all modern diaphragms are constructed of tiny blades which are adjustable, forming a larger or smaller circular opening. The larger the aperture opening, the brighter the image that is projected onto the film; the smaller the aperture, the darker the image. Standard aperture values, i.e. size of aperture openings, have been defined to allow a comparison between lenses, regardless of type and focal length. These apertures, or f/numbers, apply to any lens, regardless of whether it is used with a 35mm or medium format camera, whether it is a wide-angle or telephoto lens, or whether it was manufactured by Leitz or by Nikon. The image on the film plane will be equally bright for the same subject brightness and f/number. When we talk about lens speed we mean the amount of light allowed through the lens at its largest possible aperture. A lens with lens speed f/2.8, for example, can be opened up to aperture f/2.8 at most. An internationally standardised sequence of aperture values was devised to provide a comparable f/number sequence for manual exposure settings. This is a geometrical series of light intensities, where each aperture value is always half that of the previous value.

International Aperture (f/stop) Series

1	1.4	2.0	2.8	4.0	5.6	8
11	16	22	32	45	64	90

But the subject brightness and aperture value are not the only factors that determine the amount of light necessary for a photographic exposure. The length of time the light is allowed to act on the film emulsion is the other determining factor. The formula to calculate the exposure is therefore:

Exposure = Intensity of light x Duration of exposure

I am sure you already know that the duration of exposure is controlled by the shutter. Depending on the selected shutter speed, the amount of light will be projected onto the film surface for a longer or shorter time. It makes no difference if we call it exposure time or shutter speed, it means the same. The shutter speed, or exposure time, is also standardised for manual setting by the so-called international shutter speed sequence.

Here too, the steps are chosen so that the exposure is multiplied by 2 (or halved) from step to step. Some of the values are rounded up or down to obtain convenient numbers.

International Shutter Speed Sequence					
... 4 s	2 s	1 s	1/2 s	1/4 s	1/8 s
1/15 s	1/30 s	1/60 s	1/125 s	1/250 s	
1/500 s	1/1000 s	1/2000 s	1/4000 s		

Subject brightness, aperture value, and shutter speed, result in exposure value, but this still does not ensure that there will be the correct level of exposure. The photographic effect of the exposure also plays an important role, i.e. exposure also depends on the sensitivity of the film to the light. Film sensitivity – the film speed – was, at one time, stated in DIN and ASA values, or as is standard today, as ISO speed numbers. The larger the ISO value, the greater the film speed.

ISO Sequence for Film Speeds			
12/12°	25/15°	50/18°	100/21°
200/24°	400/27°	800/30°	1600/33°
3200/36°	6400/39°		

Again, the film speed is doubled (or halved) from one value to the next. It is possible to obtain films with intermediate values, as for example, the well-known Kodachrome 64 with ISO 64/19°.

In conclusion we can say: low subject brightness and low film speed necessitate large aperture openings and slower shutter speeds. Great subject brightness and fast film speeds require small aperture openings and faster shutter speeds.

If we consider a fixed subject brightness and a fixed film speed, then we can produce the same exposure level by opening the aperture and selecting a faster shutter speed, or, alternatively, by stopping down the aperture and selecting a slower shutter speed. Assuming you expose at $^{1}/_{125}$ sec. with an aperture of f/2.8, or at $^{1}/_{15}$ sec. at f/8, it will make no difference; the exposure, i.e. the effect on the film will be exactly the same.

The Shutter

The shutter of the F-401 is a vertical, electronically-controlled metal focal plane shutter. Because the shutter travels vertically across the shorter side of the film, and because of the special blade construction, a shutter speed of $^{1}/_{2000}$ sec. is achieved. The exposure times are produced by two shutter blinds which operate in sequence. An exposure time of 1 sec. is obtained as follows: the first blind, which covers the film completely, opens relatively quickly and exposes the film to the light. Exactly one second after the first blind was released, the second follows and covers the film. The area of the film, which was exposed first is thus covered first, ensuring a uniform exposure of the whole area, this being 1 sec. in this case. It becomes more complex for shorter exposure times: the shorter the time, the sooner the second blind has to follow the first. For example, with an exposure time of $^{1}/_{100}$ sec., the first blind starts and reaches the other side just when $^{1}/_{100}$ sec. has elapsed and the whole film frame is exposed. At this instant the second blind follows.

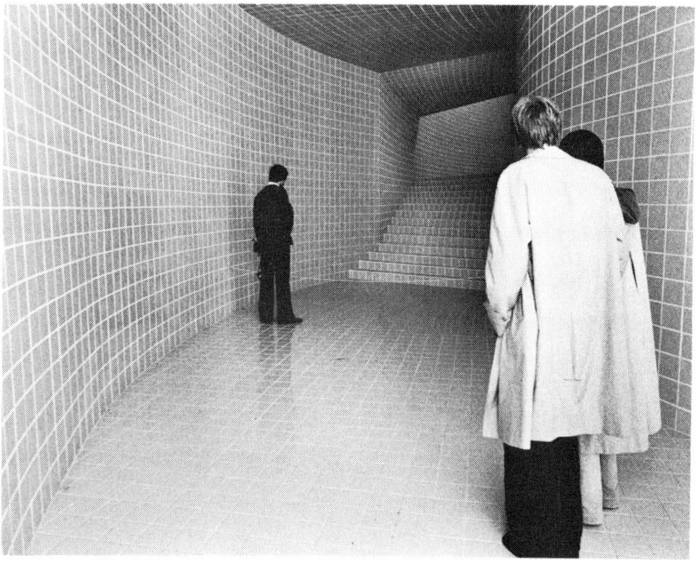

Such moments present themselves not only in art galleries; they might wait just around the corner. Photo: Rudolf Dietrich

This means that for times which are shorter than $^1/_{100}$ sec., the second blind has to follow the first even before the first has reached the other side. Thus for times shorter than $^1/_{100}$ sec. the exposure is not obtained by one single opening of the shutter over the whole area of the frame, but by a slit moving across the frame.

For the above reasons it follows that the shortest shutter speed for flash is also $^1/_{100}$ sec. The flash should be activated only after the shutter is fully open, which in the case of the F-401 is $^1/_{100}$ sec. or longer. If the flash is activated before the shutter is completely open (i.e. at times shorter than $^1/_{100}$ sec.), it would result in incompletely exposed frames.

Flash Photography with the F-401

Flash photography with the F-401 is a real joy. If the lighting conditions call for the use of the flash, the Image Master Control causes the flash symbol in the viewfinder blink. Each flash is precisely controlled by TTL (Through The Lens) metering, making incorrect exposures a thing of the past. An automatic fill-in flash mode provides the right amount of flash illumination for difficult back-lit situations. This applies whether you use the integrated flash unit by swinging the unit up to activate it, or if you use one of the Nikon system flash-guns such as the SB-15, SB-16B, SB-20, SB-22 or SB-23.

Fully Automatic TTL Flash in Program Mode

Nothing is simpler than using the F-401 in program mode, or shutter speed priority mode, with flash. In these modes the camera computer automatically sets the flash synchronization time and selects a suitable aperture and then controls the flash illumination time. In program mode, with or without flash, you need not worry about anything except composing the picture. The shutter speed priority functions in the same

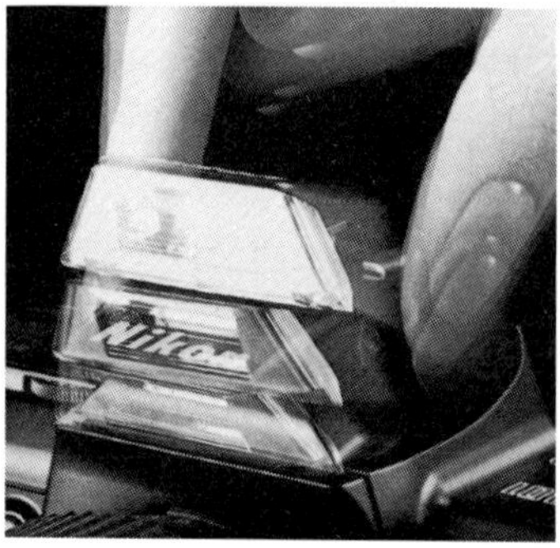

The flash need only be lifted up to be switched on. In program mode the camera computer will automatically choose a suitable aperture.

way as the program mode and I shall discuss both at the same time.

This is How You Use the Integrated Flashgun

If the red flash LED in the viewfinder begins to blink, it is a reminder from the Image Master Control that you should use a flash. If the red minus LED lights up at the same time, then the shutter will be locked because the lighting conditions are so poor that underexposed pictures are unavoidable. If only the red exposure LED is lit, then the blinking flash symbol is simply a suggestion from the camera computer to use the flash for fill-in purposes.

The integrated TTL flash is activated simply by pressing the button on either side of the unit which allows the flashgun to spring up. After about three seconds the exposure displays in the viewfinder will disappear and only the red flash LED will remain constantly lit. This means that the flash is now charged and ready to be triggered.

If the red flash LED blinks several times after it had been triggered, or if it goes out altogether after 1 – 2 sec., it means that the flash output is insufficient, because the subject lies beyond the range of the flash. The guide number of the integrated flash indicates that the range of the flash extends to about 4m. However, this range also depends on the speed of the lens attached at the time. For example, the maximum range with the AF-Zoom 35-70mm,f/3.3-4.5 is only about 3m. If you are using a film with speeds between ISO 64 and 400 you have to consider that the flash will only be suitable for portraits of a single person or small groups of people at the closer range. As fill-in flash it should also only be used for subjects up to 3.5m away. I should also mention that films faster than 400 ISO should not be used with TTL-controlled flashguns because the flash control does not function reliably for such fast films.

TTL Program Flash with Nikon System Flashguns

It is very easy to use Nikon system flashguns SB-15, SB-16B, SB-20, SB-22 and SB-23 for TTL-controlled flash photography in program and shutter speed priority modes. One of these flashguns only needs to be put in the accessory shoe and its function switch set to the **TTL** position. As previously, the viewfinder displays will go out and the flash symbol in the viewfinder lights up – the camera is now ready for shooting with flash. These very powerful flashguns have a much wider range than the integrated flash, so with an 100 ISO film for example, the range extends to at least 5m for the SB-20, and with the SB-22 you can reckon on at least 4m.

Before shooting

⚡ disappears	Recharging (with built-in flash, shutter locks; does not lock with external speedlight)
⚡ blinks	Beyond acceptable film speed range for TTL photography (over ISO 400) SB-19 or SB-E's camera selector is set to B or B (EM)
⚡ lights up	External speedlight not set to TTL

After shot

⚡ blinks (approx. 3 sec.)	Light may be insufficient for correct exposure; confirm shooting distance range

The flash indicator in the viewfinder provides the necessary information

The flash has to be set to TTL to activate the TTL autoflash in all automatic exposure modes of the camera.

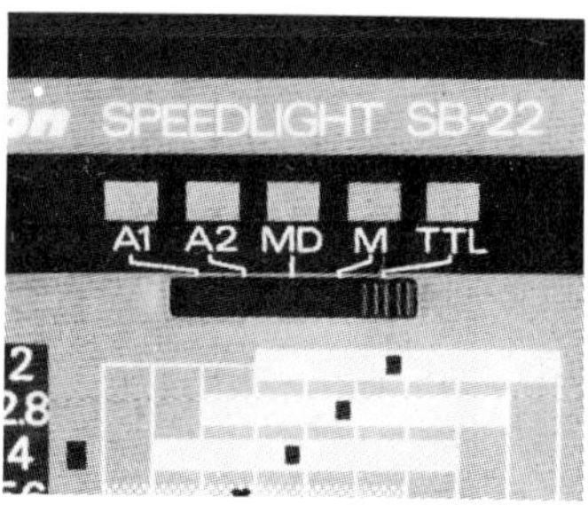

Backlit Shots with Fully Automatic Fill-in Flash

Anyone who has ever tried will know just how difficult against-the-light shots can be. If you are photographing a subject in front of a brightly-lit background with the F-401, then the main subject will be rendered considerably brighter than with other cameras because of the triple sensor metering system. But even the exposure corrections effected by the F-401 may not be sufficient to produce the ideal balance. In many cases the foreground is still not bright enough, or the background is overexposed and completely lacking in detail, and even the colours of the main subject appear rather pale because of flare.

You can avoid this problem altogether with the F-401 if you use the fill-in flash in program mode or shutter speed priority mode. With either the integrated flash or with additional flash (SB-20 or SB-22) the Image Master Control System will automatically select a suitable aperture value to adjust the brightness of the background, so that the foreground is suitably illuminated through TTL-controlled flash and the resultant picture gives a balanced impression. Not only will the colours of the foreground be realistically rendered, but the background will be shown in its natural brightness and colour.

Speed-blurred Effects with Shutter Speed Priority

If you use shutter speed priority and you set a time between $^1/_{125}$ and $^1/_{2000}$ sec., the F-401 will automatically change to $^1/_{100}$ sec. flash-synchronization time, and the resulting pictures will be just as if you selected the program mode. However, if you select times from $^1/_{60}$ sec. to **B**, then a second image will be superimposed on the flash image. This method results in some very interesting effects.

Let's assume the shutter speed has been set at $^1/_{60}$ sec. The flash will illuminate the scene for about $^1/_{1000}$ sec. (usual flash illumination time) and the image recorded on the negative will be mainly this flash-illuminated image. Then there will be another, fainter image recorded – the scene illuminated by the ambient lighting for the remainder of the $^1/_{60}$ sec. If you are photographing a moving subject, then there will be the speed-blurred trace of its movement against the core of the movement frozen by the flash. A similar effect is obtained if the sharp flash image is accompanied by an unsharp outline due to camera-movement, i.e. if the exposure time was rather long and you produced camera shake.

Most shots such as these are rubbish, but amongst them you may find the odd one which is original and effective. It is a subject area well worth exploring.

Flash in Aperture Priority

Set the shutter speed dial to **A** and the shooting mode selector on the flashgun to **TTL**. On the aperture dial select a value to suit your requirements. Should it be too dark for the autofocus to focus, and you are not using one of the AF-system flashguns (SB-20 or SB-22), then you have to change to manual focusing otherwise the release will be blocked.

If the flash symbol blinks several times after the shot has been taken, or it goes out altogether, it means that the flash was too weak, i.e. the distance too great for the flash to illuminate the subject, or the film speed was too slow, or the selected aperture number was too large. In this case you must expect the shot to be underexposed. You could try and repeat the shot with a larger aperture.

If you wish to use the F-401 in manual exposure mode with the integrated flash, or even with the additional flash in the accessory shoe set to **TTL**, then the flash will be automatically controlled by TTL control, just as in aperture priority mode, the only difference being that the selected shutter speeds between 1/60 sec. to B remain active. You will again obtain speed-blurred effects, if the subject, or the camera, moves during the exposure.

Creative Photography with Flash

If you are using one of the system units: SB-15, SB-16B, SB-20, SB-22 or SB-23, it is easy to use the flash in aperture priority mode with preselected aperture. The advantage in this mode is that you can determine depth of field for a flexible image creation, even when using flash with TTL control. If depth of field is important you can work with smaller apertures, but if you wish to have shallow depth of field you work with larger apertures, depending on whether you want to show your subject in front of a sharp background or prefer to emphasise the subject in front of a blurred background. Unfortunately you are somewhat limited in the range of aperture values by both the distance to the main subject and the film speed for which the TTL control will still function

	Film speed (ISO)					Flash range (m)
	400	200	100	50	25	
Aperture	2	—	—	—	—	4 ~ 12
	2,8	2	—	—	—	2,8 ~ 8,5
	4	2,8	2	—	—	2 ~ 6
	5,6	4	2,8	2	—	1,4 ~ 4,2
	8	5,6	4	2,8	2	1 ~ 3
	11	8	5,6	4	2,8	0,7 ~ 2,1
	16	11	8	5,6	4	0,6 ~ 1,5
	22	16	11	8	5,6	0,6 ~ 1,1
	—	22	16	11	8	0,6 ~ 0,8

The setting range of the TTL flash control with aperture priority and integrated flash.

	Film speed					Distance setting		
	400	200	100	50	25	W	N	T
Apertures	2	—	—	—	—	2.8 ~ 20	3.8 ~ 20	4.5 ~ 20
	2.8	2	—	—	—	2.0 ~ 15	2.7 ~ 20	3.2 ~ 20
	4	2.8	2	—	—	1.4 ~ 11	1.9 ~ 15	2.3 ~ 18
	5.6	4	2.8	2	—	1.0 ~ 7.8	1.3 ~ 10	1.6 ~ 12
	8	5.6	4	2.8	2	0.7 ~ 5.5	1.0 ~ 7.5	1.2 ~ 9.0
	11	8	5.6	4	2.8	0.6 ~ 3.9	0.7 ~ 5.3	0.8 ~ 6.3
	16	11	8	5.6	4	0.6 ~ 2.7	0.6 ~ 3.7	0.6 ~ 4.5
	22	16	11	8	5.6	0.6 ~ 1.9	0.6 ~ 2.6	0.6 ~ 3.2
	—	22	16	11	8	0.6 ~ 1.4	0.6 ~ 1.9	0.6 ~ 2.2
	—	—	22	16	11	0.6 ~ 1.0	0.6 ~ 1.3	0.6 ~ 1.5

● **Zoom reflector setting**

Setting range of the TTL flash control with aperture priority and SB-20

	ISO film speeds					Flash range (m)	
	400	200	100	50	25	Normal	Mit Weitwinkel-Streuscheibe
Aperture	2	—	—	—	—	3,2 ~ 20	2,2 ~ 17
	2,8	2	—	—	—	2,2 ~ 17	1,6 ~ 12
	4	2,8	2	—	—	1,6 ~ 12	1,1 ~ 8,8
	5,6	4	2,8	2	—	1,1 ~ 8,8	0,8 ~ 6,2
	8	5,6	4	2,8	2	0,8 ~ 6,2	0,6 ~ 4,4
	11	8	5,6	4	2,8	0,6 ~ 4,4	0,6 ~ 3,1
	16	11	8	5,6	4	0,6 ~ 3,1	0,6 ~ 2,2
	22	16	11	8	5,6	0,6 ~ 2,2	0,6 ~ 1,5
	—	22	16	11	8	0,6 ~ 1,5	0,6 ~ 1,1
	—	—	22	16	11	0,6 ~ 1,1	0,6 ~ 0,7

Setting range of the TTL flash control with aperture priority and SB-22 properly. The following table will demonstrate this for the integrated flash and the Nikon system flashguns SB-20 and SB-22. With average speed films and average subject distances the number of possible aperture values is greatest. The intermediate aperture values are, of course, also possible.

Fill-in Flash and Precisely Controlled Background Brightness

In contrast to the TTL-controlled fill-in flash with program mode, where the Image Master Control System balances the foreground and background based upon triple sensor metering and setting of the appropriate aperture, you are able to control the brightness of the background with fill-in flash in aperture priority mode.

By careful choice of aperture you can make the background darker, brighter, or as bright as the foreground. The brightness of the background depends on the relative brightness of the flash in relation to the brightness of the background. The main subject in the foreground will always be properly and equally well lit, thanks to the TTL-controlled flash, and this is independent of the selected aperture. How bright the background will be depends mainly on the aperture. The shutter speed will always be $^{1}/_{100}$ sec. (the flash synchronization time), and the background will therefore be brighter with fully open aperture and darker with stopped down aperture. In order to determine the aperture value for the required background brightness you first have to set the F-401 to manual exposure mode to find out which aperture value will be suitable for an exposure time of $^{1}/_{125}$ sec. to obtain the correct exposure setting. Let's assume the manual exposure setting produced aperture f/5.6 and $^{1}/_{125}$ sec. for a particular shot against the light. Now you change to aperture priority mode and set the flash to **TTL** and select f/5.6 on the aperture dial. Now you will obtain a perfectly balanced image where background and foreground will be equally bright. For a darker background you should choose in this example f/8, f/11 or even f/16. If you wish to show the background brighter then apertures f/4 or f/2.8 will highlight it more in the picture.

TTL-Controlled Multiflash

You can use more than one TTL-controlled flash with the F-401 in all automatic exposure modes. After a little experimentation you can use this to great effect; for instance, to brighten up dark areas in the background, or to simulate against-the-light scenes, and much more. As you have the TTL flash control at your service, you will be assured of perfectly exposed pictures every time!

Another bit of good news is that relatively few accessories are needed to make this possible. Apart from the extra flashgun (or flashguns) you will need one or more adapters (TTL Multiflash Adapter AS-10), an accessory shoe adapter cable (TTL Cable SC-17) and some connection cables (TTL Multiflash Cable SC-18).

To ensure that the simultaneous TTL control of several flashguns functions properly, you have to observe a few simple rules. Firstly you should only combine Nikon system flashguns. If you use flashguns from different manufacturers, you could encounter exposure problems and, at worst, even damage the camera or the flashguns. Moreover, the flash units should have approximately similar flash durations. But beware, this is not even the case with Nikon system flashguns

Fill-in flash with the F-401. The picture at the top left was taken in program mode without flash, the triple sensor metering conveyed the mood of the scene. The TTL fill-in flash fills in the main subject and adjusts the brightness of foreground and background (top right). In aperture priority mode and with TTL flash you can choose the aperture such that the background is kept lighter or darker (bottom left). Manual flash gives you precise illumination, but this is not necessarily the best picture (bottom right).

Photos: Michael Huber

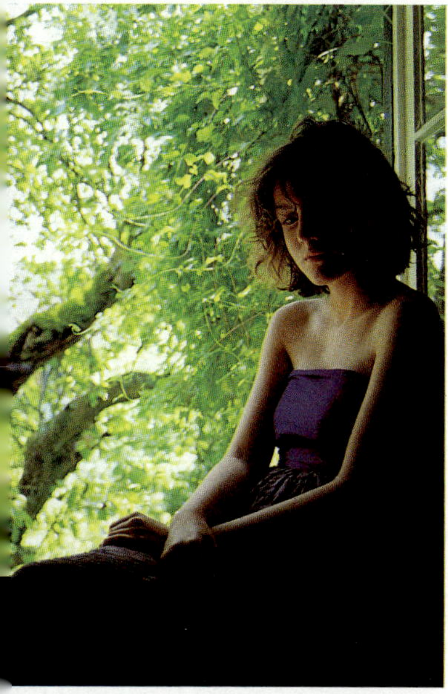
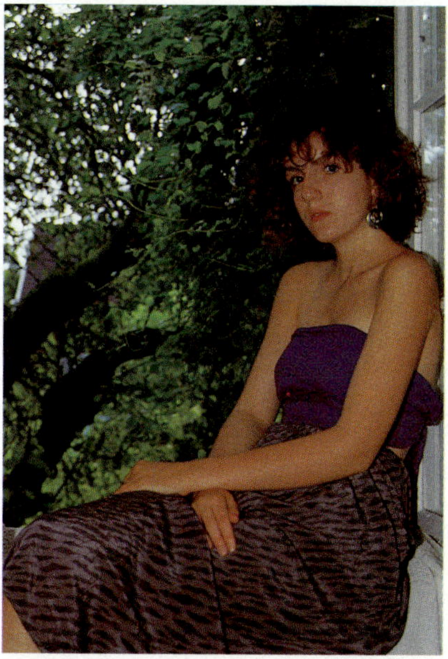
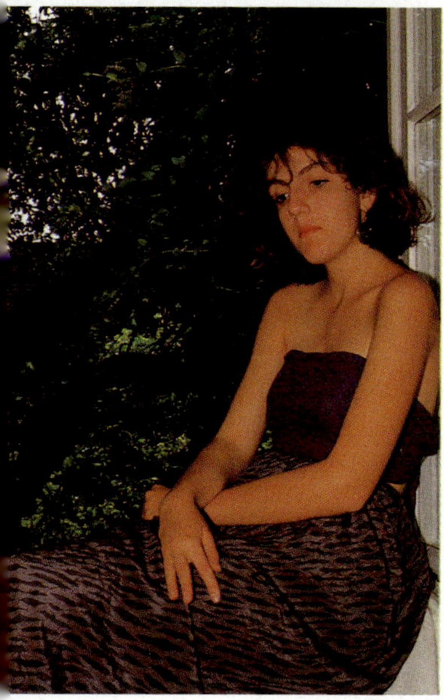
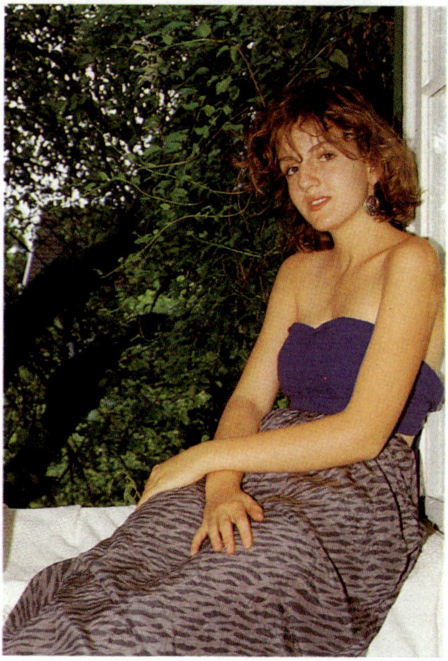

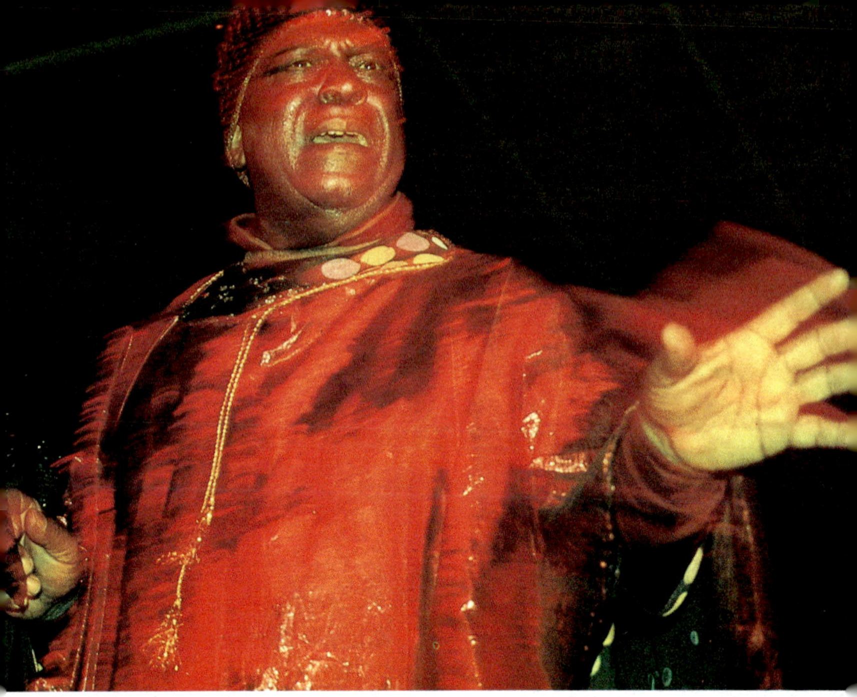

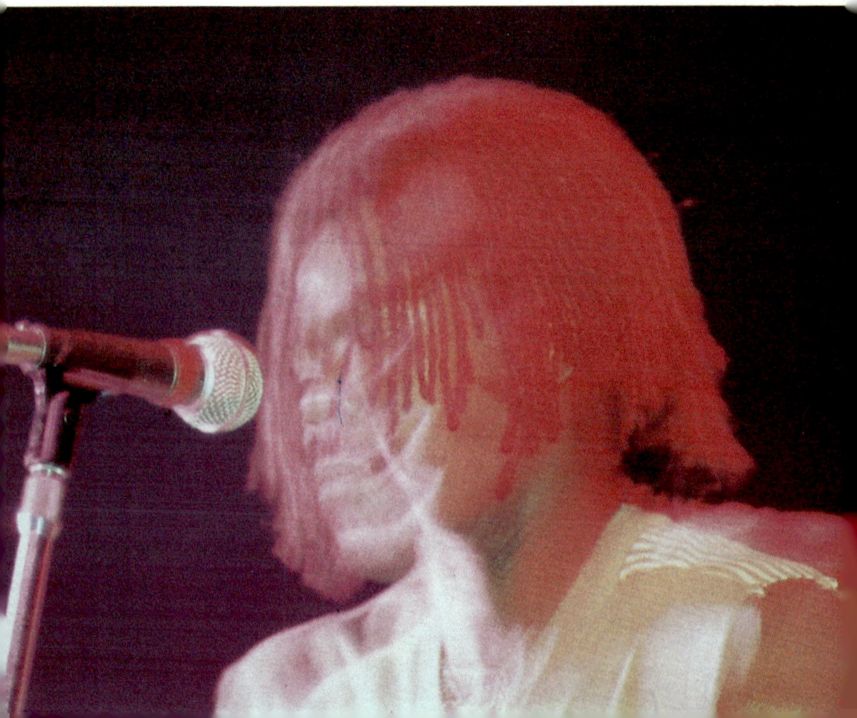

with different guide numbers. In practice this is often not critical if you remember the following general rule: –

When using multiflash always use the strongest flashgun as the main source, the weaker ones can be used for filling-in the background, for special effects, or similar purposes.

Limits of TTL Autoflash

TTL autoflash, despite all its virtues, has its limitations, and not only with regard to range. Difficulties could arise with film surfaces of different reflectivity. After all, how would you know whether Ektachrome 100 has the same reflectivity as Fujichrome 100 or Agfachrome 1000, or any other of the wide range of films available. Luckily we can generally disregard minor differences.

TTL autoflash metering is based on a calibration of a subject of average reflectivity. This calibration to the so-called average grey can have serious effects on the measurement and regulation of the flash. For example, if you are photographing dark, poorly-reflecting objects, they would be excessively brightened and would therefore look quite unnatural. On the other hand, very bright, strongly reflecting objects, would turn out too dark. The bride in front of a white wall will look too dark and the widow in black inside a dim church will be too light. In cases such as these, when you wish to improve on the automatic mode of the F-401, you have to set both the camera and the flash to manual operation.

The autoflash is also not ideal for subjects of high contrast. You will have to apply your experience and decide whether you wish to expose for the dark or for the light areas. This too is only possible in manual operation.

Both flash pictures show the "blurred effect". The sharp image is superimposed by a second, unsharp image due to the movement of the subject. The F-401 will be able to take these types of shots in both the shutter speed priority mode and with manual setting of aperture and shutter speed. In this case the shutter speed has to be set considerably slower than $^1/_{125}$ sec.

Photo: Wolf Huber

TTL autoflash of the F-401 helps you in many situations to act faster and take better pictures, and in this respect it offers one of the best systems that is currently available.

Flashguns for the F-401 – Your Choice

The Nikon System Flashguns SB-15, SB-16B, SB-20, SB-22

F-401-compatible Nikon Flashguns						
Type	**Guide number**	**for focal length, with/without wideangle diffuser**	**Batteries**	**Flashing rate**	**Flash number**	**AF flash**
SB-15	25	35/28 mm	4xAA	8 s	160	no
SB-16B	32	85-28 mm zoom reflector	4xAA	11 s	100	no
SB-20	30	85-28 mm zoom reflector	4xAA	6 s	160	yes
SB-22	25	35/28	4xAA	4 s	200	yes
SB-23	20	35	4xAA	2 s	400	yes

and SB-23 are tailor-made for the F-401. Other Nikon flash-guns can be used with the F-401, but only within certain restrictions, and are therefore not discussed here.

Flashguns by Other Manufacturers

Considering the prices charged for Nikon flashguns, it is quite understandable that you might look at those by other manufacturers. Many offer a wide range of Nikon-compatible units. If used with a system adapter, these dedicated flash-

The SB-22 flash-unit is probably the most suitable for the F-401, considering both its output and its price.

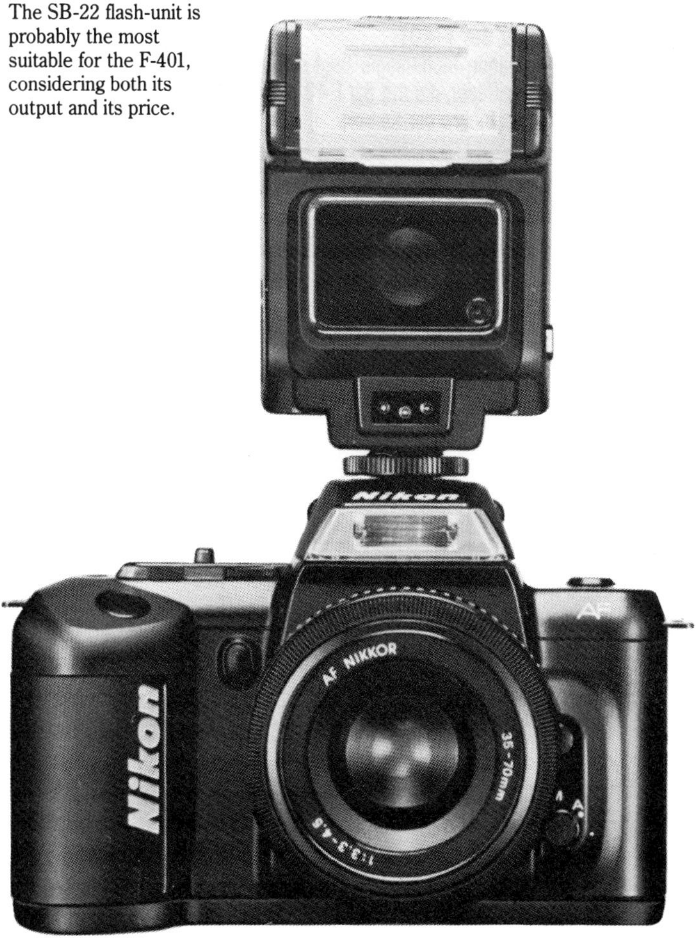

guns will work with the F-401, even in TTL flash control. SCA-300 series flashguns from such manufacturers as Metz, Braun, Cullmann, Osram and Regula are supposed to be fully compatible if used with Adapter SCA-343. However, because of the rapid change and development in camera and flashgun technology, adapters are constantly being changed. If you are not absolutely sure when buying a new flashgun, then I would recommend that you write first to the manufacturer for assurance that the particular model can perform properly with the F-401.

Then there is the question of whether buying a flashgun from another manufacturer is really worth a possible price saving. After all, the new system flashguns SB-22 and SB-23 by Nikon are reasonably priced and they also offer the facility of automatic focusing in complete darkness, which is not available with other makes. Some manufacturers also offer an AF-illuminator in the SCA-300 system that is available as an accessory. Flashguns with AF-illuminator are supposed to be available shortly from other manufacturers. However, Nikon's own flashguns should remain the first choice, as they offer all these facilities and are, as mentioned before, quite competitively priced. The SB-22 is relatively powerful, while the SB-23 is a handy unit with AF-illuminator. Before making a choice you should study the market as new units, even with AF-illuminator, are constantly introduced.

Autoflash – Only in Emergencies

If you own a camera such as the F-401 that offers TTL flash control with fully automatic fill-in flash, then you would be very ill-advised to buy one of these expensive flashguns. It is a different matter if you already own one and only use flash occasionally. With this in mind, I can offer you some tips. Push the flash into the accessory shoe and set the shutter speed manually to $^1/_{125}$ sec. Read off the aperture value for the film speed from the table on the flashgun and set this value on the aperture dial. Then you still have to check whether the subject distance lies within the range of the flashgun, by checking the table on the flashgun or in the manual, then you can release. The metering cell in the computer flash automatically measures the light reflected from the subject and controls the flash illumination time. You should generally obtain quite reasonably-exposed pictures with an autoflash.

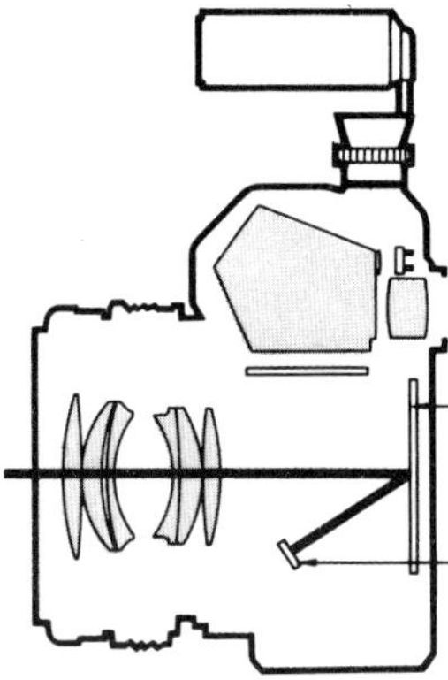

This is how TTL-controlled flash works. When taking flash photographs with system flashguns in the TTL mode the camera electronics measure the light reflected from the film surface during the exposure. As soon as it is sufficient, it switches the flash off.

This is How TTL Autoflash Works

Using the F-401 in the program, aperture priority or shutter speed priority modes, or manually, with a Nikon system flashgun in position **TTL**, the flash will be automatically controlled by TTL metering. Compared to conventional autoflash, the TTL control has the advantage that it will meter the subject properly across the angle of view of the lens. The measuring cell in an autoflash unit usually has a fixed angle of view of about 60°. This means that the measuring angle corresponds to the angles of view of lenses of 40 – 50mm focal length. If you are using a wide-angle lens with a greater angle of view, or a telephoto lens with a considerably smaller angle of view, then the values metered by the flashgun will be more or less wrong. Apart from this, most autoflash units are limited to a certain number of aperture stops, usually two or three.

The F-401 will work perfectly in TTL control with the Nikon system flashguns and other dedicated makes. Connecting the flashgun will first set the flash synchro speed to $^{1}/_{100}$ sec. If you then release the shutter the flash will fire after the mirror has been raised. The aperture will have been stopped down to the working value and the shutter blinds will be completely open. The meter cell at the bottom of the camera will then measure the light reflected from the film surface during the following $^{1}/_{100}$ sec. when the shutter is open, and control the flash illumination time according to this measured value. Therefore it does not matter whether shorter times are preselected on the camera before the flashgun is switched on. If a system flashgun is used with the F-401 in TTL flash mode, then the shutter will never be open for longer than $^{1}/_{100}$ sec. If a shorter time has been set on the camera, e.g. $^{1}/_{125}$ sec., then this will have no effect on the shutter speed when a Nikon flashgun is attached and switched on and **TTL** is selected on the flashgun. As soon as the flash is activated, the shutter speed is opened exactly for $^{1}/_{100}$ sec. However, if you are shooting in shutter speed priority or in manual modes, the shutter will also remain open for longer times in TTL flash control, if slower speeds than $^{1}/_{125}$ sec. (i.e. speeds from $^{1}/_{60}$ to **B**) have been preselected. In this case the resulting image is composed of the flash image and of a second, weaker image formed by the available light (see also the chapter on Movement-blurred Effects in Shutter Speed Priority).

Now back to TTL flash control. This is the control of the flash duration by the camera's electronics, based on the metering of the light reflected from the film surface. The selected aperture has no influence on this measurement. The different aperture values are automatically taken into account with the different selected flash illumination values. But, as with any other automatic setting procedure, this too has its limitations. After all, it does take some time, which is admittedly very short, to measure, calculate, and send the stop signal to the thyristor of the flash unit, and there is also the response time of the thyristor. If the required illumination time is significantly shorter than the response time of the equipment, then this will definitely result in overexposure. Overexposure is bound to occur with TTL-controlled flash if the distance between subject and flash is very short, compared with the guide number of the flash unit, or if the selected aperture is too big or the film speed is too great.

The solution to this is to stop down, or to use a slower film. You should also use a neutral density filter in front of the flash. Another source of incorrect exposure may be that the subject is too far away from the camera and that the amount of light that the flash is able to project is insufficient. The maximum range of the flash, which is smaller for a small aperture, and larger for a large aperture, corresponds to the flash range of the flashgun in normal manual use. It is a fact that even the best TTL flash control cannot do more than trigger the full power of the flash. If this is insufficient then you either have to go closer or you have to use a faster film.

This is How Automatic Fill-in Flash Works

The characteristics of the TTL-controlled program flash are

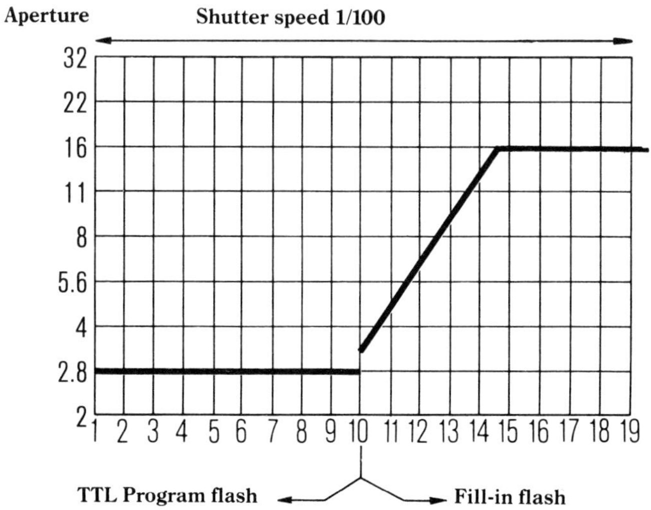

Program Flash curve. The camera computer will select a suitable aperture for the background based on the triple sensor metering result. Together with the TTL-controlled flash this results in very natural pictures with balanced fore- and background.

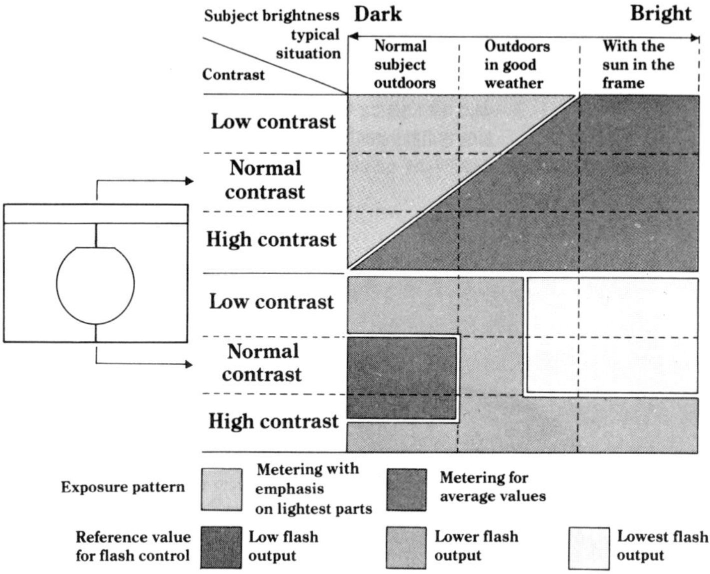

Control of the fill-in flash. Based on the triple sensor metering the camera computer reduces the flash output according to subject brightness and contrast. The final measuring is done by TTL control during the exposure.

graphically demonstrated in the following diagrams. If the average subject brightness is low (i.e. EV10 or less) then the camera computer will automatically select the largest available aperture on the lens. The shutter speed is then set, also automatically, to $^1/_{100}$ sec. and the flash illumination time is controlled by measuring the reflected light from the film surface.

From EV10 the camera computer starts to stop down the aperture in relation to the metered overall brightness and the subject contrast. Based on the triple sensor metering, and considering the shutter speed of $^1/_{100}$ sec., the Image Master Control will select an aperture so that the background is rendered naturally light. The exposure of the foreground is also illuminated by properly dosing the flash illumination and based upon the triple sensor metering. If the ambient light is bright, and the main subject in front is also illuminated by this, and also if the backlighting is not too strong, the flash output is reduced. If the ambient light on the main subject is rather weak and the backlight rather strong, then the flash will be set to a higher or full output. During the flash illumination the TTL control will ensure the fine control of the flash illumination.

By this clever method of assessing the background lighting and automatic setting of the aperture, and by automatic presetting of the flash output in consideration of the subject brightness and contrast, and relative brightness of the backlight and final TTL control, the F-401 attains very high quality in fill-in flash photography. To obtain similar results by any other means, even a professional photographer would have to take a sequence of shots to be sure of the same image quality.

In Exceptional Cases – Manual Flash

What has been said about autoflash can also be applied, to a certain extent, to manual flash. However, I can imagine only two situations where you would use a manual flash with the F-401. Either you possess a powerful manual flashgun and wish to use it on your new camera, or you are faced with a very rare and unusual shooting situation, which you can deal with better by manual setting than by TTL control. In the latter case you could use also one of the Nikon system flashguns in manual operation.

The argument that one can expose more accurately with manual flash than with any automatic flash control only applies if you also possess the appropriate know-how and are using a rather expensive flash exposure meter. Without a flash exposure meter you would have to calculate a suitable aperture for the subject distance, the film speed, and the guide number of the flash.

I shall repeat here the most important points for the use of manual flashguns with the F-401.

- ○ Set the shutter speed on the shutter speed dial to $^{1}/_{60}$ sec.
- ○ Select the appropriate film speed on the scale of your flash unit and read off the appropriate aperture setting for your subject.
- ○ Read off the aperture value on the scale on the flashgun and set it on the aperture dial on the camera.
- ○ Now you only need to release the shutter.

All this can be done quickly and easily. However, only a few subjects are entirely flat and equidistant from the camera. Most subjects have a certain spatial depth. Just think about the bride and groom's table at a wedding reception. If you select an aperture for the distance to the centre of the table, you may find that the bride in the foreground looks quite pale and washed out, mother-in-law at the centre looks nice in her new hat, but only the nose of the person at the end of the table glows out of the darkness. Even if you bounce the flash off a white ceiling the results may be unpredictable. So what aperture should you choose? Compared with manual flash the use of TTL autoflash is more convenient and far more precise.

Of Guide Numbers, Apertures and Distances

Thanks to TTL autoflash, the field of flash photography is now open to anyone, without the need for complicated calculations and settings. Even so, the dedicated amateur photographer will still be interested to learn all the basic rules. This comes in useful from the start when you are trying to decide what flash outfit to buy. Should you go for the one with guide number 32, or is guide number 30 just as good? Would you have known that a flashgun with guide number 32 would require a flash distance only 25cm more at an aperture of f/8?

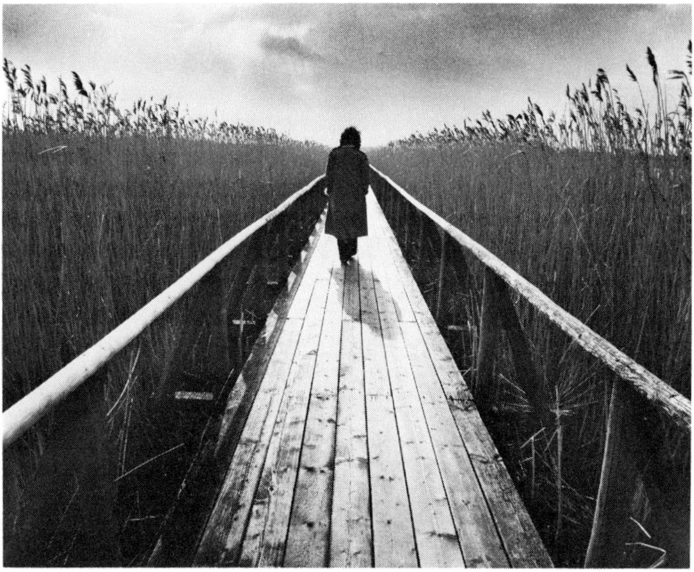

The wide-angle perspective emphasises the spatial depth. To obtain the large depth of field you have to focus on the foreground and stop down (in aperture priority mode). Photo: Rudolf Dietrich

The guide number is the value which takes into account the parameters which have a bearing on the exposure level. The law that brightness decreases as the square of the distance applies to flash photography. If we have a subject at 1m distance from the flash, another at 2m, and a third at 3m, then the subject at 2m distance will only be one quarter as bright as that at 1m, and the one at 3m distance will be only one-ninth as bright as the first. That is what is expressed by the guide number. The guide number depends not only on film speed, but also on the brightness and hence the distance of the flash from the subject. If the distance of the flash from the subject is known, the aperture required may be calculated by knowing the guide number of the flash:

$$\text{Aperture} = \text{guide number} \div \text{distance}$$

The distance at which a subject may be correctly illuminated at a given aperture and flash output may be calculated as follows:

$$\text{Distance} = \text{guide number} \div \text{aperture}$$

For example, if a subject at 2m distance is illuminated properly with a flashgun with guide number 32 and an aperture setting of f/16 ($^{32}/_{2}$), then the same subject at 4m distance would have to be taken at aperture f/8 ($^{32}/_{4}$) to obtain the correct illumination level. If we look at this the other way round, an aperture setting of f/4 will expose a subject correctly at 8m distance and for an aperture of f/11 the correct distance is 2.9m.

Most flashguns have a scale from which you can read off the correct distance for a given aperture. The guide numbers given always refer to a film speed of ISO 100. Higher speed films result in a higher guide number and therefore a greater range for the flash for the same given aperture. This information is also given on the scale of the flashgun.

In the case of autoflash units and TTL autoflash the guide number represents the maximum output of the flash. If the subject or the distance requires less illumination, the automatic metering will regulate this by reducing the flash duration. Most of us will be glad that the autoflash has released us from this cumbersome calculation.

Flash Tailored to the Subject

There is hardly a subject that is not suitable for flash photography. The only limitation is the size of the subject and the output of the flashgun. It should be quite obvious that it will not be possible to illuminate an entire church, a market square by night, or a large gym with the normal Nikon system flashguns. With normal subjects, however, you should not encounter any problems with Nikon system flashguns as they will illuminate between 5 – 12m, depending on the automatic exposure mode.

Family Snapshots

One of the most frequent subjects is the snapshot for the family album. Whether it is a birthday party or a happy family reunion, most of these pictures are taken indoors and at distances between 1.5 to 4m. Lenses with focal lengths between 28mm and 100mm will be the most useful for these situations. To complement them, a flash with a guide number of 20 and films with speeds of ISO 100 or 200 should cover almost any situation. When pointing the flash directly at the subject you have to take care that the distance differences of the various objects are not too great. As the illumination decreases as the square of the distance, the foreground could be too bright, or if the foreground is correctly illuminated, the background could be too dark. Even if you use TTL autosetting, it will be difficult to find the right compromise, especially if you are working with slide film. Try to bounce the flash from the ceiling as this usually produces good results and works perfectly with Nikon system flashguns, whose reflectors can be turned to various angles.

To avoid unnatural looking portraits, place a diffuser in front of the flash to soften the light and bounce the flash as well. If your flash has no diffuser you could loosely attach a piece of tissue paper to the flash reflector. A flash mounted directly on the camera is particularly unsuitable for portrait photography. The integrated flash of the F-401 is even worse. It often results in the well-known "red-eye" effect. This is caused when the axis of the lens and that of the sitter's eyes are in line and the light is reflected from the back of the eye. If there is an angle between the subject and the flash axis, then the red light is reflected away and no longer registers in the picture. To avoid these "red eyes" you should bounce the flash. If this is not possible, a diffuser will reduce this unpleasant effect. However, either one of these remedies will reduce the effective flash illumination, always depending on subject distance.

Architecture

For interior architectural views you will need a powerful flash to illuminate large areas, and a flashgun with a guide number of 30 may not be adequate in this case. Space may be limited and you will almost certainly have to use a wide-angle lens. This in turn will necessitate the use of a wide-angle diffuser in front of the flash. This too reduces the effective power of the flash.

Sport and Action

Telephoto lenses dominate in the field of sports photography. As well as flash you should also use faster films (note, however, the upper limit for TTL autoflash with the F-401 is 400 ISO), together with a tele-adapter to concentrate the light of the flash. Be aware, however that flash is often not allowed at sporting events.

Portraits and Still-life Photography

Portraits and still-life in studios usually require powerful flash output because rather slow, fine-grained, films are normally used. The illumination has to be arranged to be uniform and to avoid deep shadows and harsh contrasts. A reflector screen will change a hard flash into a softer light source. An additional white or silver reflector screen (cardboard covered with aluminium foil, polystyrene board or similar) will reflect light into the dark areas. A background of the appropriate lightness or colour will add the right mood to your composition.

The most controlled results are achieved when you use **multiflash**; that is more than one flashgun. Three flashguns should cover any conceivable situation. The strongest flash is usually positioned more or less in front as the main illumination, and for some subject themes it might be positioned as top-lighting. If you are not using a flash reflector, you could substitute a large sheet of transparent paper which you could hang about one meter distant from the flash, between the main subject and the light source. A special diffuser foil is equally suitable of course. A second, weaker flash can be used to lighten the background to the required degree or to fill-in from below. The third flash could be used to pick out or emphasise specific areas. Your flash equipment will not be provided with modelling lights, as is the case with studio equipment, but this need not worry you. Two cheap clip-on lights using 60-watt reflector bulbs should serve as perfect modelling lights.

Similar arguments apply to **table-top photography**. Only here we have smaller objects and uniform illumination can be achieved by some different tricks. The secret here is a light tent made of transparent paper or plastic foil, illuminated by two flashes, one on the right, the other on the left.

Copying is best done by using two matched flash units, positioned on the right, and the left, at 45°. The distance to the picture to be copied, for sizes up to DIN A2, should be about 80cm. Diffuser foils are also recommended for this application.

Macro Photography

Actual macro photography is best done with multiple flash. The SB-15, the SB-20, and also the SB-22, with a multiflash cable and a multiflash adapter are suitable for this application. If the intensity is too great you could use a neutral grey filter foil.

For TTL-controlled macroflash, Nikon specifies minimum aperture values for flash distances of up to 60cm, depending on film speed. If a larger aperture than the recommended least value is selected, then the reaction time for TTL control may be insufficient for exact control of film illumination time.

Speed → / Flash distance ↓	ISO 50	ISO 100	ISO 200
	Least aperture value		
25 cm	11	16	22
50 cm	5,6	8	11

Slide Duplication

Duplicating slides with flash has proved very successful. However, one limitation is that the TTL auto control becomes ineffective because of the low nominal speed of slide duplicating film. You will have to experiment with various distances of the flash or by using various neutral density filters to test for the best conditions. For slide duplicating it is necessary to use colour filters such as those by Kodak or Hama.

Autofocus is very suitable for close-ups such as these. This hibiscus flower was taken with the AF Zoom 35-70mm,f/3.3-4.5 at a focal length of 70mm and automatically focused from a distance of about 15cm. To obtain maximum depth of field you should select aperture priority with an aperture of f/11. In case the resulting shutter speed is too slow, put the camera on a tripod. *Photo: Wolf Huber*

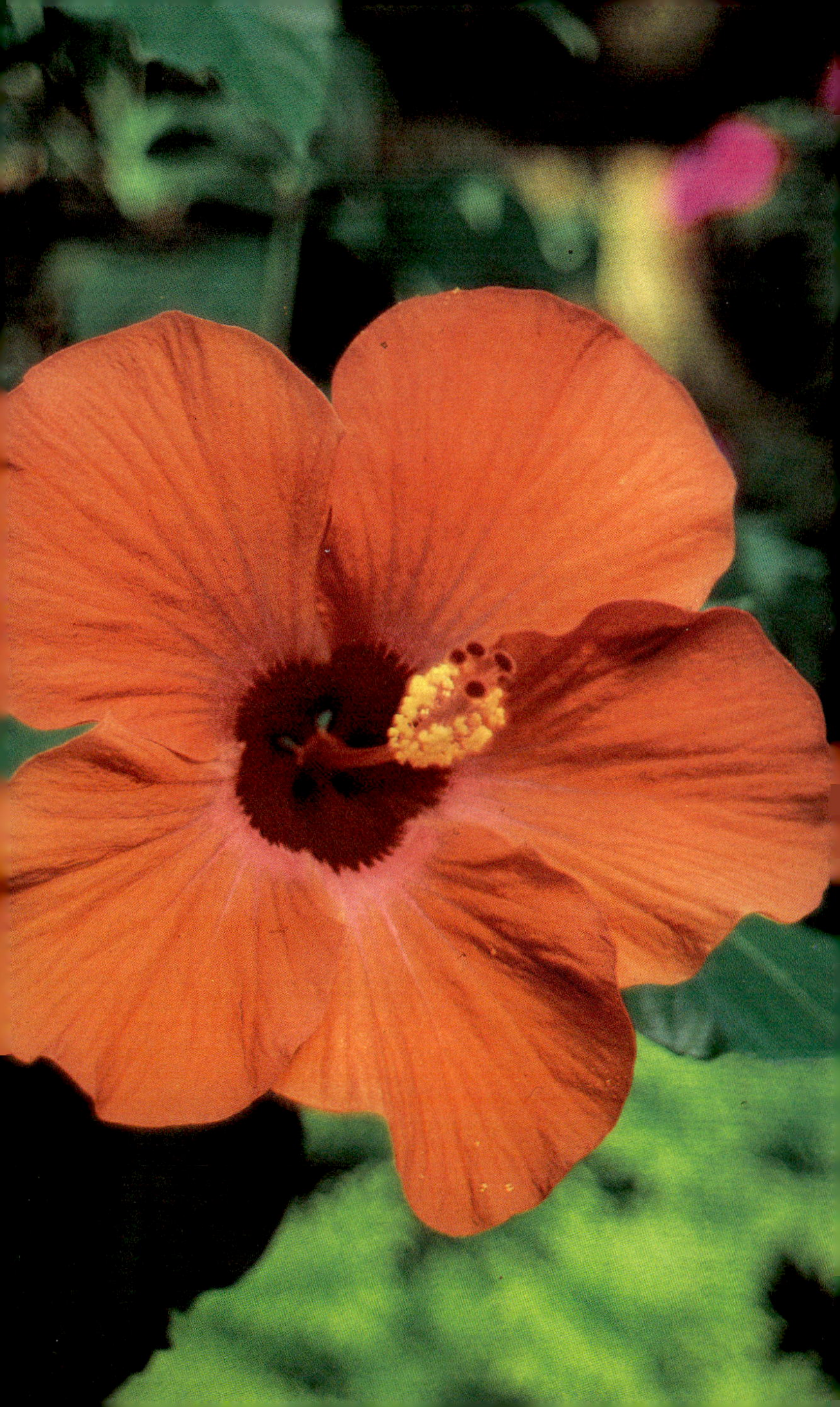

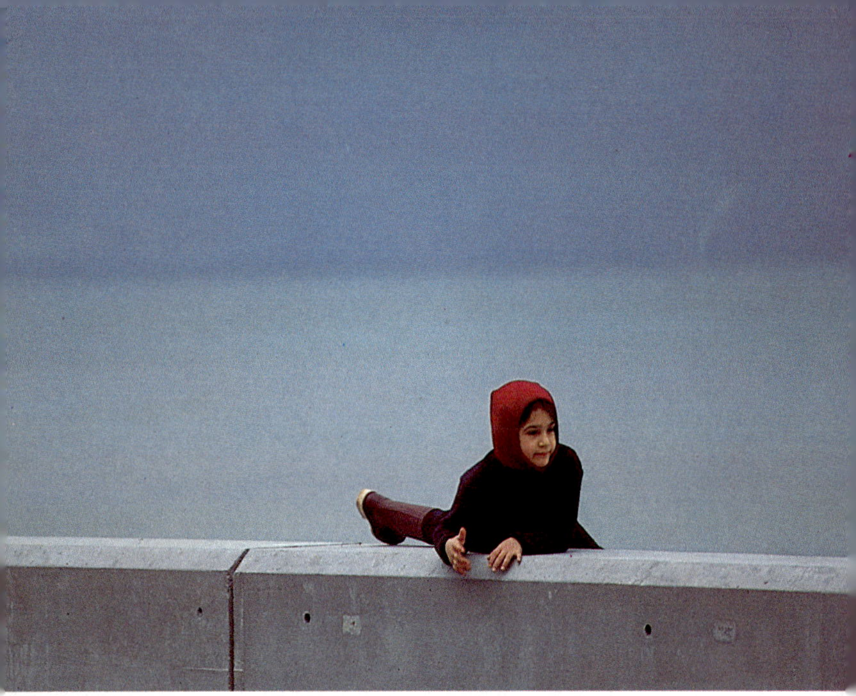
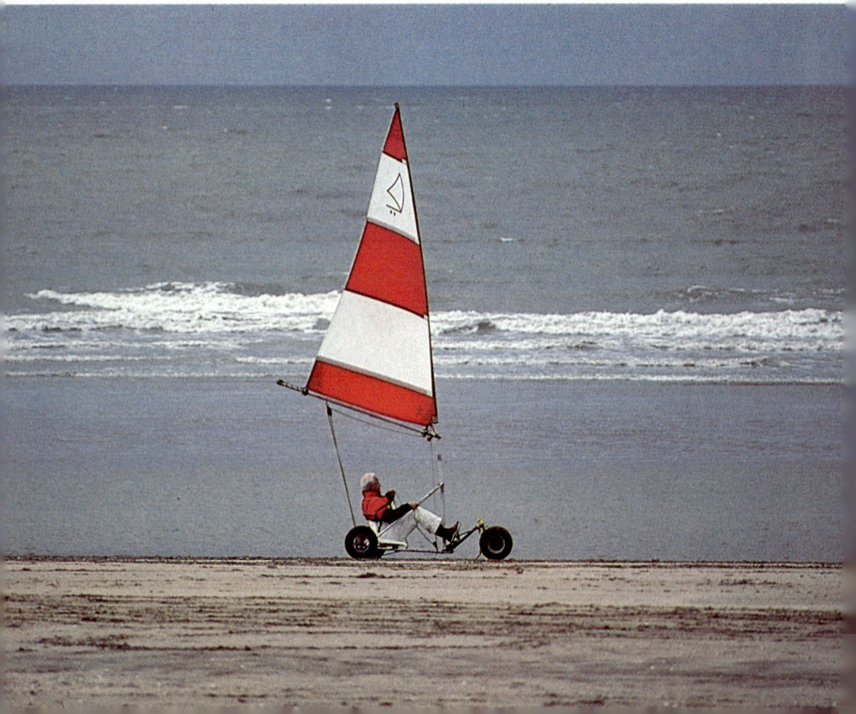

The Correct Lens for Every Subject

One question that is asked repeatedly is: "What lenses should I buy to be able to take good pictures?" To such a question I can only answer that cause and effect is put the wrong way round. The pictures are always shot by the photographer, not the lens. My answer in such a case is: "What do you want to photograph and what are your particular aims?" Only when you are clear about your photographic ambitions can you decide on the equipment to serve your creative intentions. Then you can decide, after knowing the characteristics of the various lenses, and subject to your budget, which is the right lens for your needs.

The Focal Length Determines the Character of the Lens

The different angle of view of different focal length lenses determines the characteristic differences in the change in reproduction scale for the same subject distance. The normal focal length of a modern 35mm camera is about 50°, which has an angle of view roughly corresponding to that of the human eye. Lenses with focal lengths of 40mm and less, e.g. 35mm and 28mm, are considered to be wide-angle lenses. Focal lengths of 24mm, 21mm, 18mm and even 16mm are generally referred to as super wide-angle lenses.

Wide-angle pictures, taken from the same viewpoint, i.e. the same distance from the subject, differ from pictures taken with standard lenses in that they contain a lot more, i.e. they have a considerably larger angle of view. This in turn also

---

Grey sand, grey concrete wall, no sunshine – not a suitable subject for the photographer, you say? Both of these pictures, taken with the 200mm focal length lens, prove the above assertion wrong. *Photos: Wolf Huber*

means a smaller scale of reproduction. The spatial impression is also changed. However, if you enlarge a portion to the size corresponding to that which a normal standard lens would have shown, you will see that the perspective is the same at the same distance from the subject.

By reason of their construction, wide-angle lenses, at full aperture, suffer from a much greater decline in illumination from the centre to the edge than do standard lenses. This effect increases with decreasing focal length. However, this has been corrected to a large extent in Nikon lenses. In addition, for the super wide-angle lenses there are also very noticeable distortions which are particularly apparent at the edge of the picture. These too are greater, the shorter the focal length of the lens. If we compare pictures at the same scale of reproduction, then we find that the wide-angle view shows a different perspective from that of the standard lens. The items in the subject closer to the camera are emphasised in size with respect to a diminished background. We can regard pictures which make use of this characteristic as typical wide-angle views.

Lenses with focal lengths of over 55mm are generally called telephoto lenses. Photos taken with these lenses cover a smaller angle of view, but the reproduction scale is larger – the subject is drawn closer. In addition, the depth of the subject is compressed by the more distant viewpoint and it looks flatter. Fast telephoto lenses with good reproduction qualities are quite difficult to construct and are therefore also quite expensive.

Standard Lens for Reportage

I doubt whether you will make a good photo journalist if you always take your pictures from a safe distance with a telephoto or zoom lens. Just look at pictures in a photographic gallery, or at collections of shots from photo journalists in the fifties and sixties. You will notice that there are a lot of pictures which give you the feeling that you are there yourself. This is due to a large extent to the skill of the photographer, but it is also a result of the perspective given by the standard lens which was used then by the majority of photographers for most situations. It was not the fashion to simply zoom in from a distance. Rather, as a famous *Life* reporter said: "get closer to the subject!" This is still true today and it is quite obvious if we consider that pictures taken with a standard lens from close to the subject will have maximum impact.

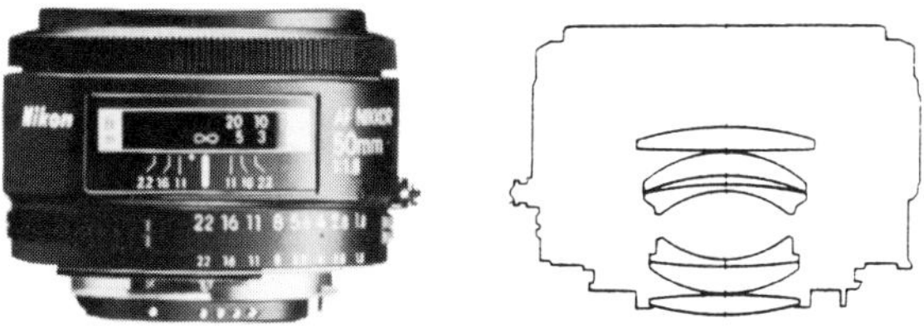

The AF Nikkor 50mm,f/1.8 has all the good qualities of a standard lens: great speed, good reproduction quality, compactness and reasonable price. These advantages have to be added to the fact that the standard lens has an angle of view similar to that of the human eye.

We could say that the standard lens will produce realistic pictures of its own volition. Provided, of course, that you are not trying to show a view from an unnaturally close, or distant, viewpoint. Then there is another important point: no other focal length has such high speed as the 50mm lens. The greater speed is not only useful for available light photography, in addition it offers the possibility of sharply reducing the depth of field. As we mentioned previously: the larger the aperture, the smaller the depth of field and the better you can show the subject against a blurred background. Considering the choice of available Nikon AF lenses, then the fixed focus AF 50mm,f/1.4 must be first choice. It not only offers excellent sharpness, it also has very high speed. The 50mm,f/1.8 seems less attractive to me, not because it does not offer excellent quality, but, on balance, I would go for the "standard zoom", the AF 35-70mm,f/3.3-4.5, if the reduced lens speed is of no consequence. The macro fans amongst you will perhaps choose the AF Macro 55mm,f/2.8, which offers a very high performance for this focal length range.

Wide-Angle Lens for Architecture and Landscape

The normal wide-angle range starts with 35mm and includes the 28mm lens. From 24mm, including 21mm and sometimes even the 28mm, these are called the super wide-angle lenses. At present Nikon offers no shorter AF-lens than the 24mm for the F-401. Wide-angle lenses are, as the heading indicates, particularly suited to general-view pictures. No other lens will show a landscape to better advantage than a good wide-angle lens. Whether you are showing rugged mountains or an endless flat desert, both types of view will be best served by the wide-angle lens. The wider angle of view gives the observer the distinct impression that he is there himself. Also for interior photography, whether you wish to show a living room or a large hall, the wide-angle lens is ideal. Often you cannot get far enough away from a subject with a standard lens. It is not only this physical restriction that makes this lens less useful, but a view of a room with a wide-angle lens looks more natural. After all, we normally first look around when we enter a room, and the view from a standard lens is almost a ''technical error'' as it gives the impression of a sectional view. Of course, this is fine if it was the intention.

From a given distance the wide-angle lens will include more on your film than the standard lens, but, as mentioned previously, you only need to enlarge a certain section of a negative and the difference is lost. The perspective is therefore only seemingly different from that of the standard lens for a given distance. It will change only when you take the wide-angle lens close up to the subject. If you go close enough to your subject to produce the same reproduction scale as that of the standard lens, then you will get quite different pictures. Not only will you see more in the picture than on the one with the standard lens, the perspective will appear distorted. In a portrait the nose, and especially the tip of the nose, will appear unnaturally large, while the ears, further away from the camera, will look unnaturally small. This example presents quite an impossible impression, but you can use the wide-angle lens to great advantage in showing certain impressions. After all, you usually intend to show and emphasise one particular aspect against the rest, the background. Particularly in landscape photography where you want to draw attention to a characteristic building, a tree, animals or people in a relatively emphasised foreground against a spacious, less emphasised background, a wide-angle lens close to is the only way to do it. If you wish to take landscape or interior architecture, then you will need an AF wide-angle lens. At the moment this means only the AF-Nikon 24mm,f/2.8. However, I am sure Nikon will produce in the near future a 20mm lens for the F-401. Even though there are some problems with automatic focusing for the extremely short focal lengths, this would be acceptable, if only the automatic exposure control would function with one of these AF wide-angle lenses.

Exposure Problems with Wide-Angle Lenses

When taking pictures with a wide-angle lens you have to consider that the light reading could be quite misleading as the wide angle of view is not covered by the standard focal length. You could check this by taking the same subject in the open, on a tripod and taking two shots, one with the wide-angle, the other with the standard lens. With the standard lens a bright sky will cover only a small section on the edge, which only makes a small contribution to the light reading, but with the super wide-angle, the sky suddenly covers half your picture.

The F-401's Image Master Control will compensate for this to a certain extent. Even so, in many cases you will take home underexposed pictures. In such a situation you should point the camera to largely exclude the sky from the frame, and activate the AE-L button. Now you can re-align the camera and release, having excluded the excessively bright sky from the general measurement. In extreme cases you could manually store the metering change to manual exposure and result without sky. Now it makes no difference whether the sky covers 20%, or even 80% of the picture, the choice of frame is entirely yours.

Ideal for Portraits – The Short Tele Lenses

The focal lengths between 85mm and 105mm can justly be described as portrait lenses. These focal lengths are ideal for portraits because even if you arrange for the face to fill the frame, you have enough distance between the camera and your model not to crowd in too much. Faces appear particularly natural with these focal lengths. If you tried to take a portrait full-frame with a standard lens, you would have to move very close to your subject and the perspective distortion would be quite apparent. Therefore you would have to move away with a standard lens and then enlarge the required section from your original frame. If you then compared the result with a portrait taken with a 85mm tele the latter would be the better picture. Nikon has at last brought the AF 85mm,f/1.8 onto the market. This is a very fast portrait lens, at a relatively favourable price, that should suit even professional requirements. In addition there are a number of zoom lenses that cover this focal length.

Good for Action Photography – The Medium Range Telephoto

Whenever there is something going on and you are not able to move close to the action, then it is handy to have a telephoto lens up to 200mm at the ready. Under certain circumstances it is quite an advantage to photograph from a distance. You maintain the overall view of busy scenes and pick out the sort that catches your eye. If you now manage to catch the rider falling off his horse, or a super backhand at tennis, or children at play, you are always ''with-it'' with the telephoto lens. Nikon offers, with the AF-Nikkor 180mm,f/2.8 IF-ED, a lens that not only focuses precisely and quickly, thanks to internal focusing, but also offers exceptionally high reproduction quality, thanks to the use of special glasses. One serious disadvantage though: its price makes the price for the F401 look silly. Viewed in this way, you will probably choose the 70-210mm,f/4.0 AF-Zoom and be very contented.

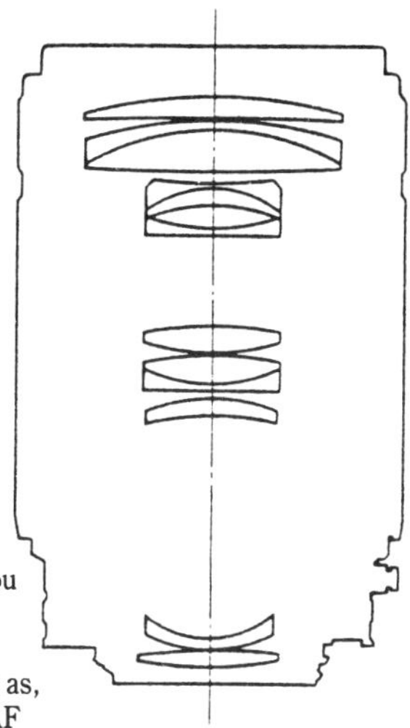

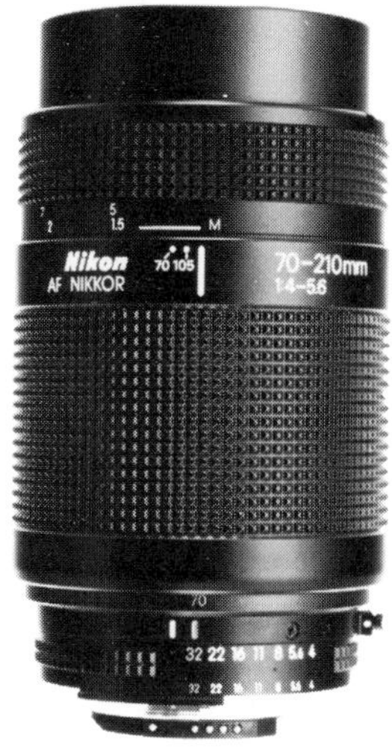

In the medium telephoto range you will find some reasonably priced Nikon lenses such as, for example, the AF 70-210mm,f/4.0-5.6.

Stalking your Subject – The Long Lenses

Long lenses over 200mm are almost out of the question for the amateur photographer. The really good lenses in this category are heavy, very expensive, and not very handy. The professional sports and animal photographer needs these long lenses as part of his basic equipment. The general amateur photographer will generally have to think twice before investing in one of them. The new Nikon AF 300mm,f/4.0 may just about lie within the realm of possibility. I would not recommend trying a cheaper, non-AF lens. As mentioned previously, neither the autofocus, nor the exposure control, will work on the F-401. Manual focusing should be no problem, but the exposure metering in the camera will be inactive. However, one well-known manufacturer has already produced a reasonably-priced AF 600mm,f/5.6 lens for other makes, and a Nikon-compatible version is likely to follow.

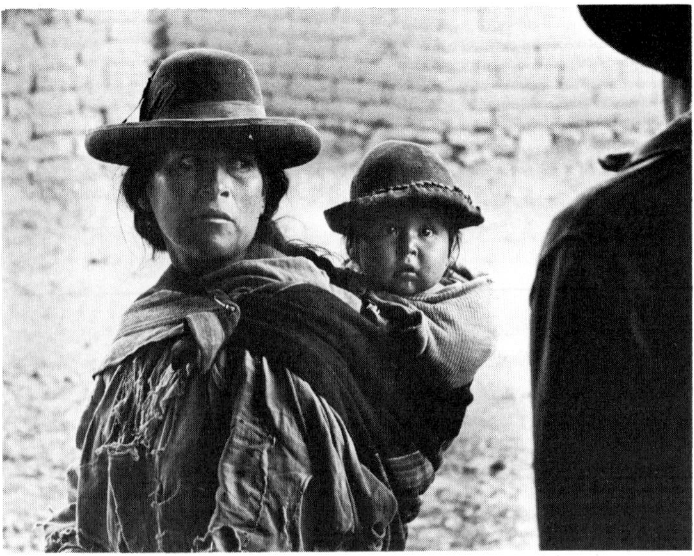

A medium telephoto zoom to about 200mm belongs in your travel bag, and then you can take such a shot from an unobtrusive distance. Photo: Rudolf Dietrich

Lenses and Accessories for Macro Photography

Whether you photograph coins, stamps, flowers or stones – when taken from very close range these objects have a very special attraction. No wonder that this type of photography is becoming increasingly popular, even with the amateur. But where macro-photography begins is a debatable point. Strictly speaking it starts with a reproduction ratio of 1:1. In general terminology most people will accept reproduction ratios from about 1:4 as macro photography.

The most important points in macro photography are good illumination of the subject, exact focusing, and as large a depth of field as possible. With the F-401 only aperture priority, or manual exposure, is to be recommended. In macro photography you should never work without complete control over the aperture. There is, of course, also the problem of camera shake and therefore the necessity for fast shutter speeds. The use of a tripod is one way of coping with these restrictions. Extension tubes, bellows, and the entire Nikon program of AF-unsuitable lenses, cannot be used with the F-401 as the exposure metering is inactive, as mentioned previously. This will not stop you taking close-ups with the F-401, but you will have to use AF-lenses, where you have the advantage of automatic focusing which is critical in this range.

Supplementary Lenses – a Simple Way to Start Macro Photography

Supplementary lenses are the simplest and cheapest possibility if you want to enter the field of macro photography. They are screwed into the filter thread of your lens and reduce the focal length. You can move closer to the subject and thereby increase the reproduction ratio. For the 52mm filter thread Nikon offers supplementary lenses of +0.7, +1.5

and +3 dioptres. Depending on lens and focal length you can get down to a reproduction ratio of 1:2 with this arrangement. If you are using supplementary lenses you have to stop down as much as possible to compensate for the decline in reproduction quality, which is inevitable whenever you are using supplementary lenses. Moreover, in macro photography, the depth of field is minimal and you will have to stop down for this reason alone. In my experience the AF lenses are quite suitable for macro photography with supplementary lenses. However, the automatic focusing will work only if you manage to find the exact distance range to the subject within which focusing is possible. Or, in other words, the autofocus will work with supplementary lens only if you could have focused manually in the same distance range. I would suggest you first try focusing manually, find out within which distance range the subject can be brought into focus, then change over to autofocus. After that the autofocus will work faster and more precisely then manual focusing.

Close-ups with the AF Macro Lens

The fastest and most reliable equipment for macro photography is without doubt an appropriate macro lens. Nikon has prefixed their Nikkor lenses in this range with "Micro". These macro lenses are quite normal lenses, but their design is optimized for the close range. The inclusion of floating elements causes the optimum correction to move from the infinity to the macro range according to the focusing distance.

For the F-401 there is at the moment only one AF-compatible macro lens available: the AF Macro 55mm,f/2.8. This is an excellent lens with which you can continuously focus from infinity to 0.23m (corresponding to a reproduction ratio of 1:2). For the macro fan this would not be a bad choice as a standard lens for the F-401 because it is also perfectly suited for normal photography by reason of its special correction.

What Lenses for the F-401?

The lens tables at the back of the book list all Nikon lenses that can be used with the F-401. However, this does not mean that they are all actually recommended. From the range of lenses available, there are eight AF zooms, two AF wide-angle, four AF telephoto, two AF standard lenses and one AF macro lens, that are actually fully suitable for the F-401. All the automatic exposure and shooting modes available on the F-401 will work perfectly with these lenses. The reason for this is the electrical contacts on the new AF lenses, which are used to convey information between the lens and the camera computer. Compared with the F-501, where the lens functions are electrically and also mechanically transferrable, which also allows the use of conventional Nikon lenses with fully functionability of all exposure modes, the F-401 has no mechanical transfer facility. Because of this extra facility, the F-501 is also more expensive than the F-401. Nikon invested the saving in doing away with conventional information transfer in better user-convenience by introducing the Image Master Control. The only disadvantage is that this makes the F-401 more or less incompatible with previous Nikon lenses.

If any lenses other than AF lenses are used, the automatic focusing by AF function is inoperable. This would be acceptable, but the non-function of the exposure metering is the real problem. If you are using your old Nikon lenses with the F-401, you have to set the shutter speed manually on the shutter speed dial, and the aperture has to be set on the **aperture ring of the lens**. To obtain a light reading you have to use a separate handheld exposure meter. My special tip: use one of your fully-functional AF lenses in manual operation to obtain an exposure reading and suitable shutter speed and aperture value. Set these values on the aperture dial and shutter speed dial of the F-401. Now you can insert the conventional Nikon lens, set the previously-determined aperture value on its aperture ring. You can now release. Whichever way you do this, it is quite cumbersome and you will agree with me when I say that conventional Nikon lenses are not to be recommended with the F-401.

If you already own some Nikon lenses and a camera, then you can use them with the above restrictions on your F-401. There is one advantage that may console you somewhat: if you are using an old Nikon lens, with a speed of f/5.6 or faster, then the AF-function in the F-401 will assist you during manual focusing. As soon as you have focused the subject perfectly, the green in-focus LED in the viewfinder will confirm this by lighting up.

Should the limited range of lenses presently offered for the AF system be a problem (a 18mm or 21mm wide-angle and a 90mm or 100mm telephoto would be a welcome addition), then you can use one of the conventional lenses. However, we can be reasonably sure that Nikon will complete the range of lenses for the AF system fairly soon. My own enquiries at well-known lens manufacturers have revealed that some of them intend to complete the range within a few months and introduce their own models.

Quality Means More Than Lots of Elements

How many elements are arranged in a lens and whether this has been worked out by computer, or with an old-fashioned slide rule, is of no consequence to the photographer. What is of importance is the optical quality, i.e. what sharpness and brilliance a lens is capable of producing. Nikon is one of the manufacturers who has played an important part in the development of cameras and lenses in the past 25 years. I shall give you here a short insight as to how this previous experience and technical know-how has been utilized in the development of the new AF Nikkor lenses.

Nikon was amongst the first manufacturers who managed to optimise their lenses with equal success for both the close and the far ranges. This was a great step forward, because

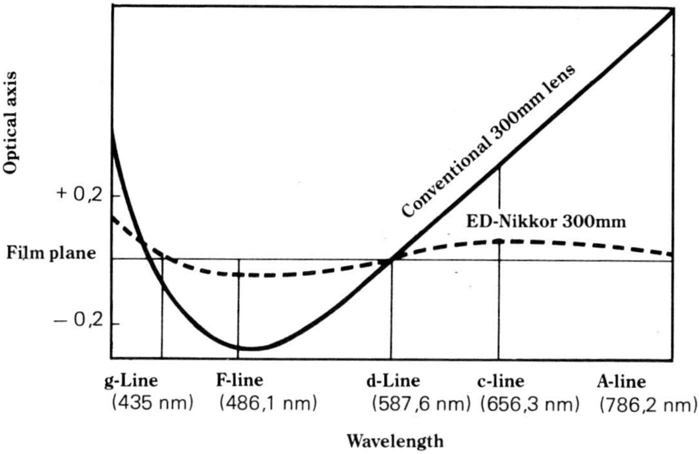

In conventional lenses the plane of focus of the different spectral colours, i.e. the different wavelengths, do not coincide and therefore do not meet on the film plane. This is corrected to a large extent in the Nikon ED lenses.

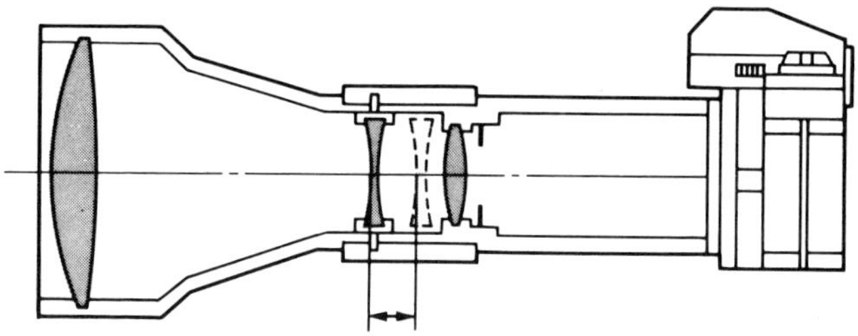

A modern Nikon lens with internal focusing. Only one relatively small member moves within the lens tube. The overall dimensions of the lens are slimmer and lighter. These excellent qualities of construction, ED glasses with their exceptional dispersion (ED), and internal focusing (IF), are utilized in the new AF lenses.

conventional lenses are generally optimized for use at infinity. This means that any errors are least when the lens is focused on infinity; the reproduction quality is at its best. By incorporating so-called close-range correction (CRC) Nikon makes some of their lenses suitable for close-range photography. This is achieved by the use of additional movable elements which compensate to a large extent for certain typical close-range errors, such as curvature of field. The CRC lenses incorporate such a design in which an additional group of elements move in relation to the two outer groups. These experiences have been utilized in the construction of the Nikon zoom lenses as are offered today in the Nikon AF system range.

Nikon's achievement in the field of special correction for telephoto lenses is quite exceptional. Chromatic aberration plays a considerable role in long focus lenses. Blue, green and red light is not combined to a common focal point, which results in colour fringes. These days all modern telephoto lenses are achromatic, that is chromatically corrected to a certain extent, and actual rainbow fringes are quite rare. But this does not constitute real contour sharpness by a long way; only apochromatic lenses can achieve that. The optical precondition for their construction is the use of special types of glass, so-called ED glasses, which have extremely low dispersion. Their use in the overall lens construction results in the sum of chromatic aberration being close to zero.

In the matter of focusing Nikon has also been in the forefront. In conventional telephoto lenses the whole lens moves whilst focusing, which alters the overall length of the lens assembly quite considerably, because the focusing movement in conventional lenses is longer, the longer its focal length. If you are handling a very long lens this could be quite difficult and cumbersome. If you are in a hurry, you will usually end up with some sort of approximation. Nikon's secret for solving this problem is internal focusing (IF). The overall length of the lens remains constant, and focusing is achieved by moving the optical member between the two main groups. Not only can you focus more quickly and accurately with these types of lenses, they are also lighter and more convenient. This renders the focusing movement extremely short. Such lenses can be easily and quickly focused both manually and by autofocus function. Furthermore, this construction can easily be combined with the automatic correction (CRC), which produces an overall improvement in reproduction quality. Because of these advantages Nikon offers the two new AF telephoto lenses, the AF 180mm,f/2.8 and the AF 300mm,f/2.8 with internal focusing.

Fixed Focal Length or Zoom?

If you own a good camera you will also want to buy a few good lenses for it. But which, that is the question. One zoom for everything, is just about the worst advice anyone could give you. To be sure there are several arguments in favour of the zoom: you need not change the lens during shooting, which is faster and less distracting; you need not carry several lenses around with you as one all-in lens is cheaper than the sum total of several individual focal lengths. But almost all these arguments can be countered. One zoom lens can be so cumbersome and heavy that you might as well leave it at home. If you are using a zoom, you would not try to get the best viewpoint, but stand in one position and just simply twiddle your controls. Pictures don't get any better in this fashion.

A zoom lens, whose picture quality is anywhere near that of a fixed focal length lens, can cost the earth. The present state of technology is capable of producing a zoom lens, using special types of glass, special lenses, floating elements, and fine precision mechanics, that has the same quality of reproduction as high-quality fixed focal length lenses. Even maximum aperture, weight, and overall dimensions need not be much worse, comparing quality with quality, than the bulkier and heavier of the two fixed focus lenses, usually the longer extreme of such a zoom. There is only one thing wrong with the argument – nobody would be able to afford such a super zoom. This is the reason why zoom lenses generally available have much slower speeds and why the optical problems which arise in the construction are still corrected by including

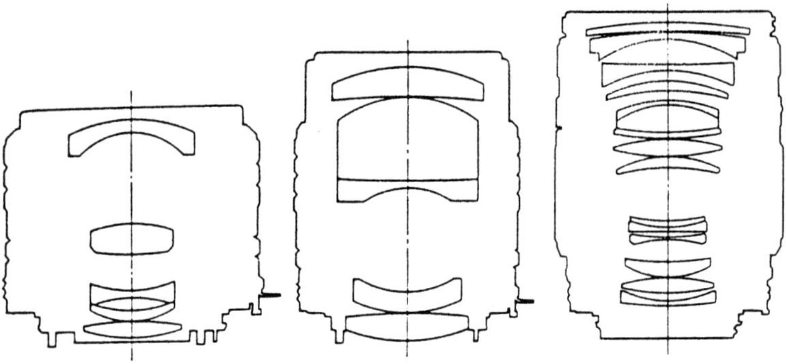

These diagrams demonstrate the advantages and disadvantages of zoom construction. The fixed focal length lenses require only five elements in their construction (35mm,f/2.8 on the left and 105mm,f/2.5 centre). The AF Zoom 35-70mm,f/2.8 requires fifteen elements and consequently is heavier, larger and, despite the considerable optical expenditure, more susceptible to flare and reflections.

extra elements. In this way a fixed focal length lens with nine elements becomes a zoom with fifteen and more. Even if this extra expenditure in elements compensates for the errors, the zoom will never produce better results than a fixed focal length lens. One has to keep in mind that every extra element has two additional air/glass surfaces and however much multi-coating is used, the lens will lose contrast and become more susceptible to flare when more elements are used in its construction. Even the recent trend towards lighter, faster, and above all, smaller zooms, which is also the case for AF lenses, must be a regressive step from the point of view of optical performance. Don't ever ask for the maximum number of individual elements when you decide on a lens – it does not mean that you are getting value for your money. I suggest you read several magazines where you can usually find comparative lens tests. For my own part I usually decide on the one with fewer elements between lenses that have been assessed as equally good.

Situations where the light is poor, with just a few artificial light sources, present no problems to the F-401, thanks to triple sensor metering. Whether in a museum, or an amusement arcade, you can expect to get a well-exposed picture. *Photos: Wolf Huber*

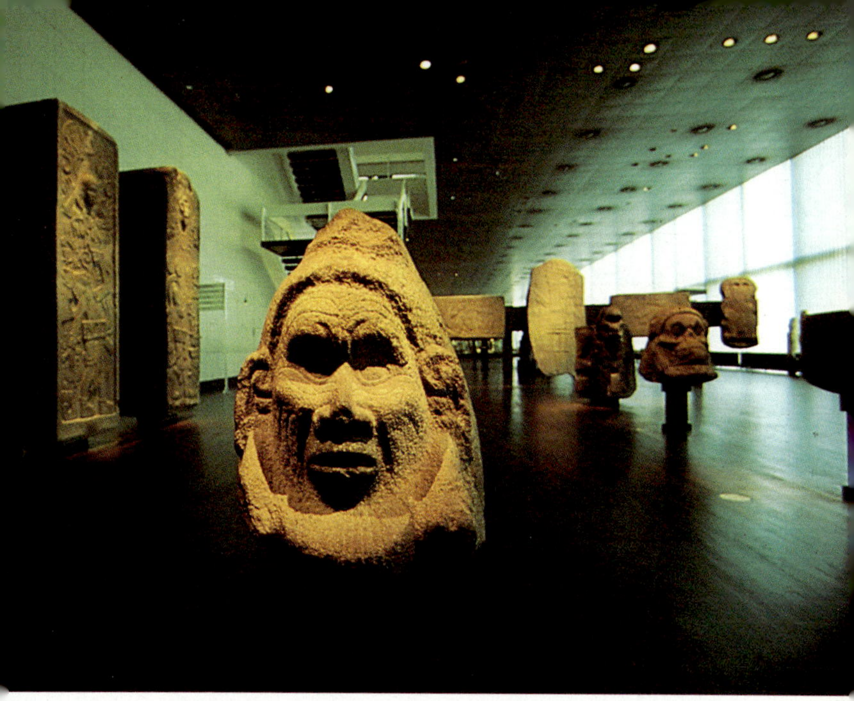
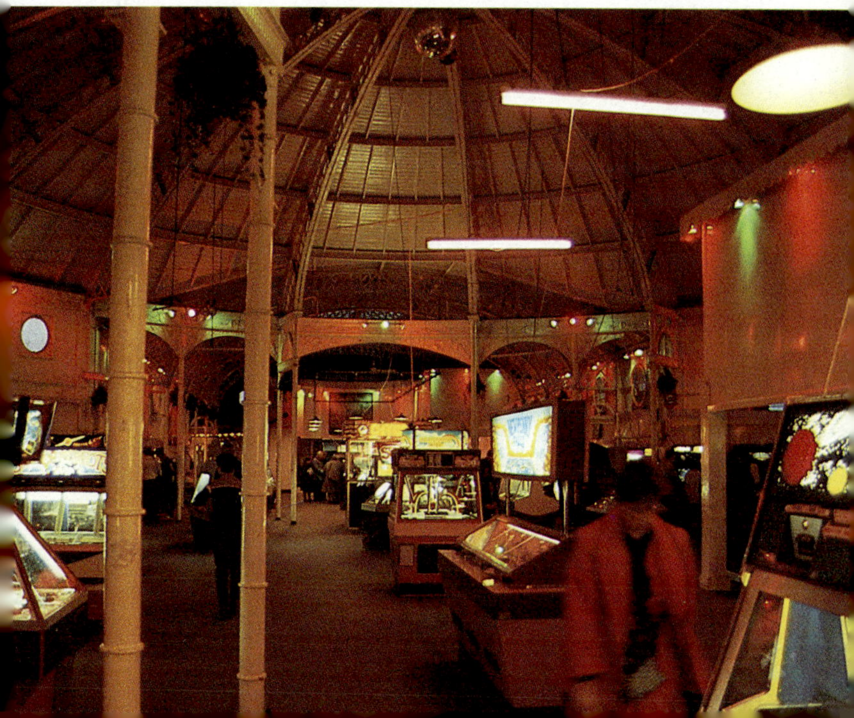

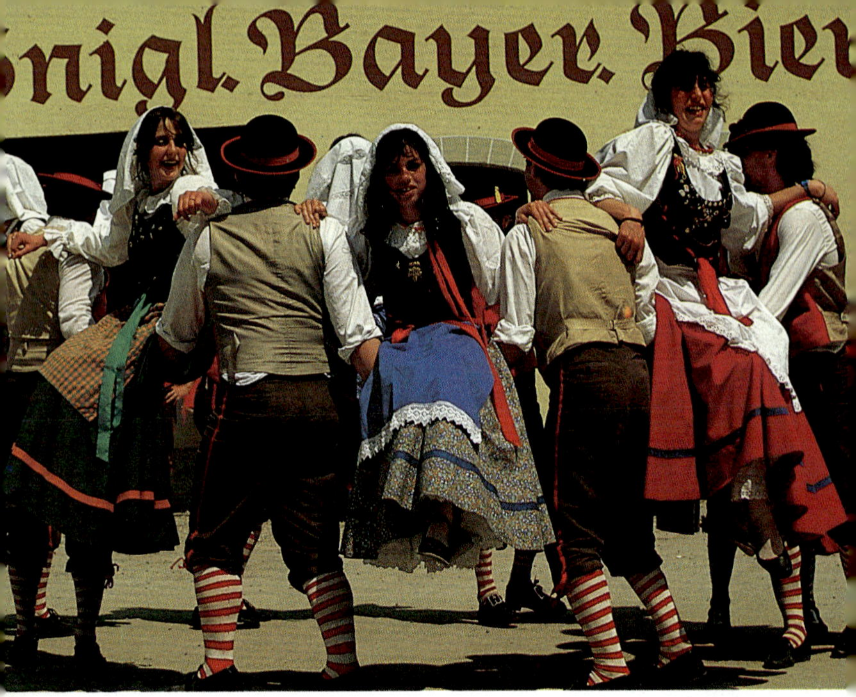
Bayer.

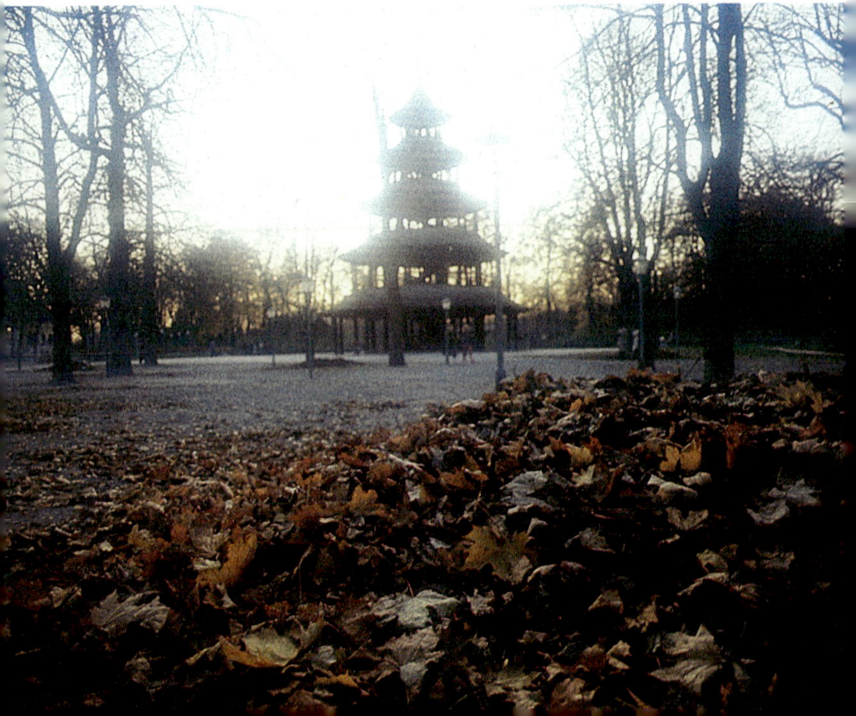

In conclusion we can say, every zoom – and the same is the case for fixed focal lengths – represents a compromise between range of focal lengths, lens performance, speed, weight, size and price. Except that the technical effort required is not so extensive with fixed focal length lenses as with zooms and, at least in theory, their price should be more reasonable. Or the other way round, at the same price, the fixed focal length lens will be technically more refined because the basic technical cost for a zoom lens is already that much greater. Another aspect to consider is that modern zooms are produced in greater production runs than fixed focal length lenses and may therefore be relatively cheaper. But the basic pricing levels vary from manufacturer to manufacturer. An expensive fixed focal length lens from one manufacturer need not necessarily be better than a reasonably priced zoom from another. Don't make the mistake of dismissing either one or the other out of hand. One thing seems certain, for optimum quality at a certain focal length, you would be best served by a fixed focal length lens.

Should We Consider Lenses from Independent Makers?

As far as AF-lenses are concerned there will be no alternative choice for some time for the F-401 user. As soon as the reputable manufacturers offer Nikon-compatible AF lenses, then they will certainly be worth considering. One thing is clear, good quality has its price. Be cautious before you are taken in merely by the price. There are a number of cheap offers about, but as far as I know, some have caused trouble and even damaged the F-401.

This shot of Bavarian folk dancers was an "automatic success" in program mode with autofocus, either with ISO 200 or ISO 400 film and a medium telephoto lens. The autumn view in the park was taken with a wide-angle lens from a crouched position, focusing on the foreground, and a small aperture ensured large depth of field. *Photo: Wolf Huber*

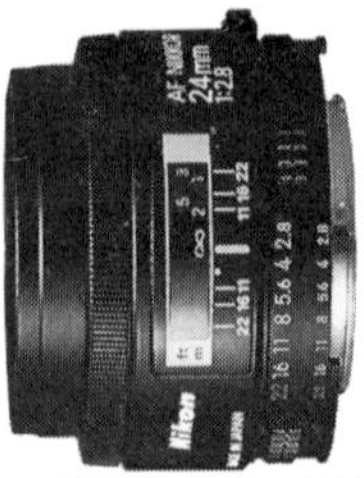

AF Nikkor 24mm f/2,8

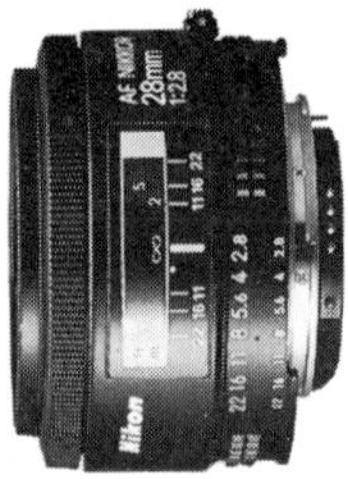

AF Nikkor 28mm f/2,8

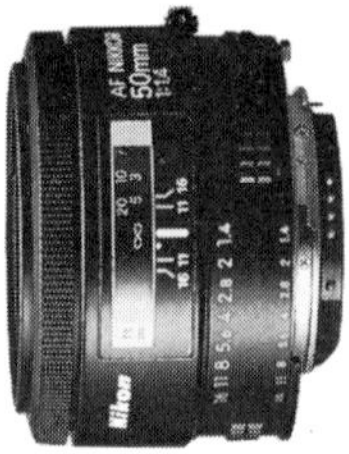

AF Nikkor 50mm f/1,4

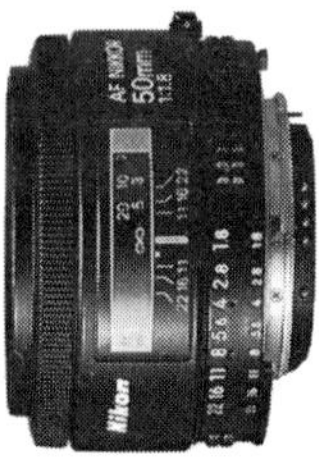

AF Nikkor 50mm f/1,8

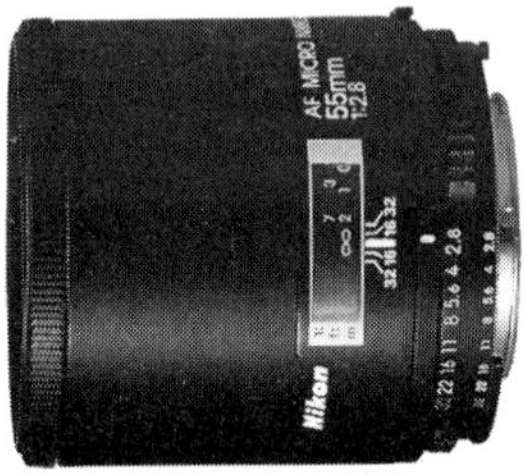

AF Micro-Nikkor 55mm f/2,8

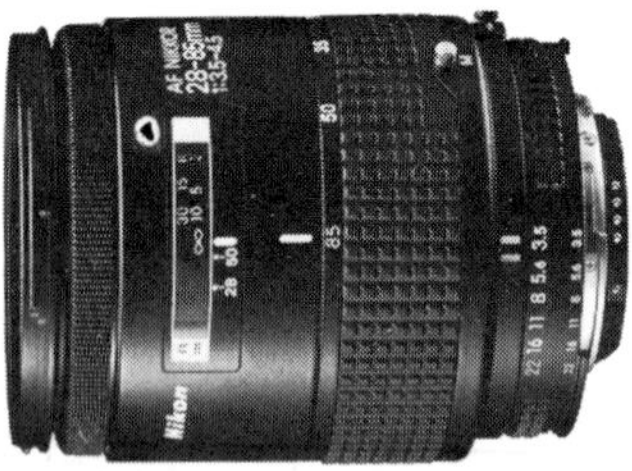

AF Zoom-Nikkor 28–85mm f/3,5–4,5

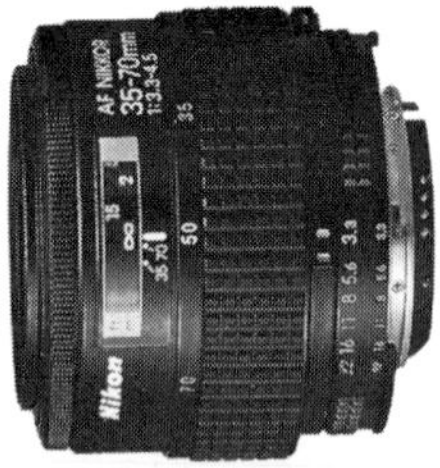

AF Zoom-Nikkor 35–70mm f/3,3–4,5

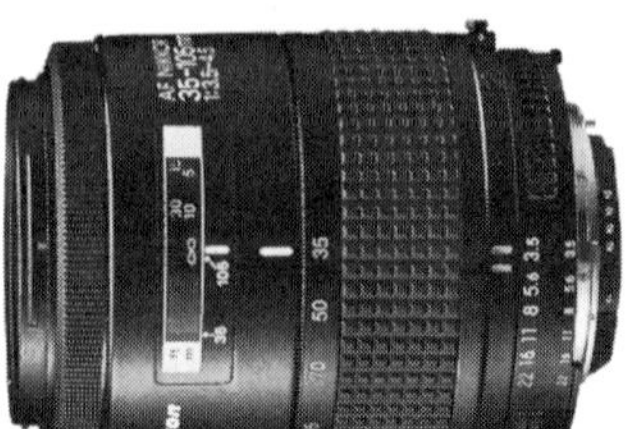
AF Zoom-Nikkor 35–105mm f/3,5–4,5

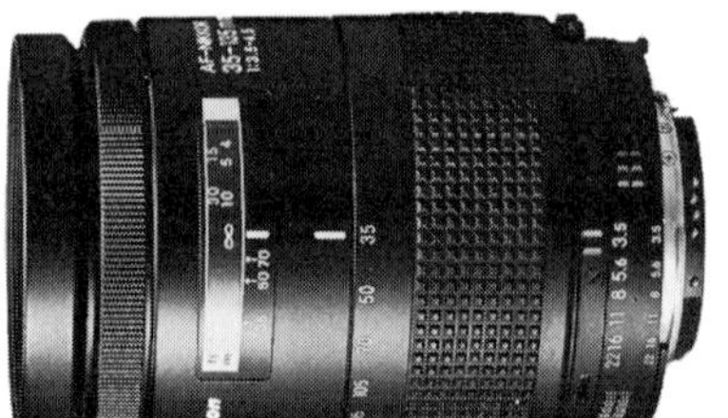
AF Zoom-Nikkor 35–135mm f/3,5–4,5

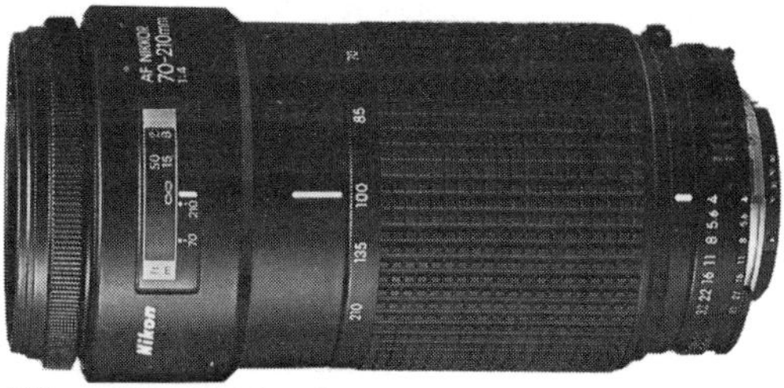

AF Zoom-Nikkor 70–210mm f/4

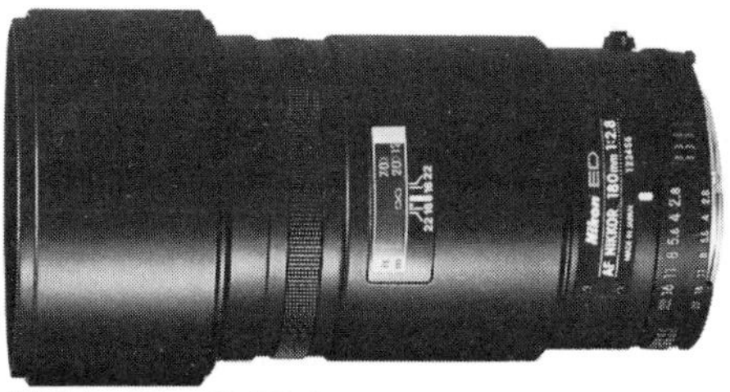

AF Nikkor 180mm f/2,8 IF-ED

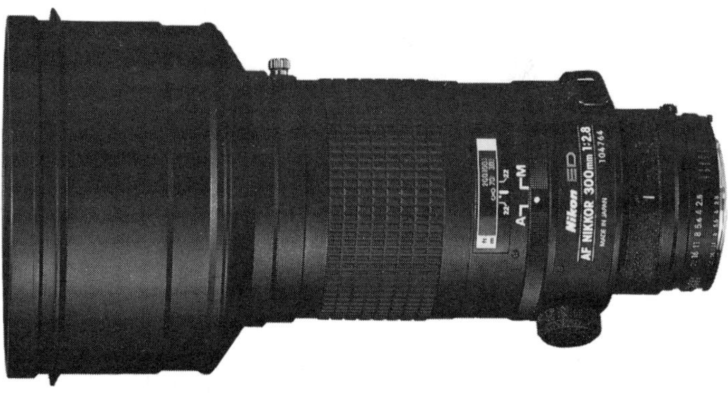

AF Nikkor 300mm f/2,8 IF-ED

An overview of Nikon AF lenses currently available. The selection is quite reasonable at the moment and it is hoped that Nikon will complement it in the extreme wide-angle range (see table at the back).

Nikon, of course, will only furnish warranty for their own lenses used together with the F-401. That they do not give you any guarantee that other lenses will work perfectly with their own cameras cannot be held against them. Should you eventually decide on a Nikon AF-compatible lens from a reputable manufacturer, then your risk should be minimal. SIGMA, for example, offer two Nikon-compatible AF zooms, the 28-70mm,f/3.5-4.5 and the 75-200mm,f/3.8. If the manufacturer gives you a six-year guarantee, then such a purchase would be worth considering.

The Ideal Lens Combination

It does not exist! However, there are criteria which should assist you in deciding which lenses would make an outfit to suit your own particular needs. Before you go and buy one or two zoom lenses, you should first consider lens speed, handiness, weight, and price, and compare these with the fixed focal length lenses. I am sure you will come to the conclusion that fixed focal length lenses, in the range from 28mm up to 50mm, are almost always lighter, faster, and even cheaper, than a good zoom. The AF Nikkor 28mm,f/2.8 weighs only 269g and measures 4.6cm. The Nikon AF Zoom 28-85mm, f/3.5-4.5, on the other hand, weighs 500g and measures 8.9cm. As you can see, the fixed focal length lens in the wide-angle range is more than an aperture stop faster and much easier to carry. If we now consider the longer focal lengths, around 180mm, then the fixed focal length lens still has the advantage of being faster, but in respect of handiness and weight, the AF Zoom 70-210mm,f/4.0 is better than the AF 180mm,f/2.8. In the latter case the optical superiority of the 180mm lens is worth considering.

My advice for the novice is this. Buy the AF f/1.4 standard lens or the AF Zoom 35-70mm,f/3.3-4.5 for your F-401. Later, when you know better where your preferences lie, you can complement the standard lens with fixed focal length lenses

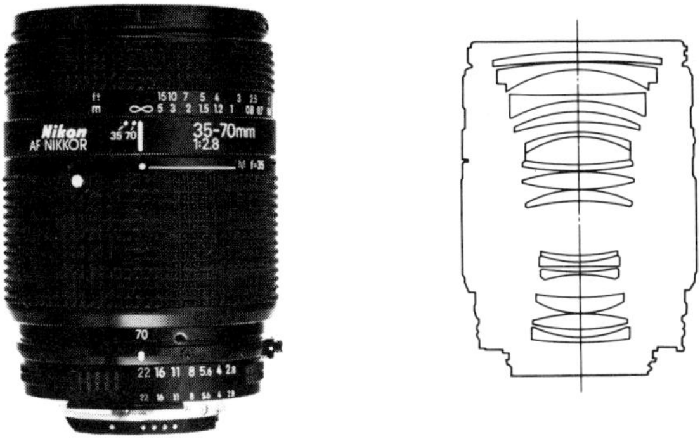

The AF 35-70mm,f/2.8 is particularly fast and a very useful ''standard zoom'', which is complemented perfectly by the AF 70-210mm Zoom. Do consider, however, whether some fixed focal length lenses in the wide-angle and telephoto ranges would not be the better solution.

in the wide-angle range or further AF zoom lenses. How about the 24mm AF-lens for landscapes and the AF Zoom 70-210mm,f/4.0 as universal telephoto lens? Then there is also the super-telephoto AF 300mm,f/4.0 to be added to the list. Perhaps SIGMA will bring out a 400mm,f/5.6 in Nikon AF-compatible construction.

Who says you have to buy the whole outfit at once? Or do you think you can't take any good pictures because you don't have a complete range of lenses? One good quality lens is always worth more than two inferior ones, specially if they are safely tucked away at home.

Useful Accessories

I cannot help smiling when I see some so-called photographers laden down by their gadget bags full of "essential" gear and hear them say proudly that they managed to take three shots. On the other hand one can also make the mistake of taking so little equipment on holiday that you are insufficiently equipped for any situation. The secret lies in finding just the right balance to be suitably equipped for any foreseeable situation without having to take a donkey to carry it all.

A UV Filter and a Lenshood are Essential

A UV filter, or a skylight filter, should always be on the lens. Both protect the lens against scratches and fingermarks and cut out harmful UV. The UV rays could cause blur and fogging. Both the UV and the skylight filter absorb UV radiation. The skylight filter also prevents excessive blueness in cloudy conditions, on the beach, in the mountains, or if the sun is high in the sky. Personally I find excessive blue hue more unacceptable than the warmer rendition of colours that the skylight filter gives me. But this is a matter of taste, but the purists amongst you would probably choose a UV filter.

As mentioned above, either one of these filters will protect the front element of the lens. It is definitely much cheaper to have to buy a new filter. To have to buy a new lens because it is scratched would be a severe blow.

Another essential item to be fitted to all your lenses is the lenshood to protect against flare. The image on the film should be formed only by the light that stems from the subject. If light enters the lens from the side it could be reflected by the internal surfaces to create flare and cause poor picture contrast and weak colours. If you take a photograph directly into the sun, then a lenshood would be of little use. In practice lenshoods of hard plastic or metal are better than those made of rubber. The flexible hood can easily get folded back in the heat of the moment, and then you find you have some inexplicable vignetting in some of your pictures. Flexible hoods are more practical only when you store your camera.

In any case, never allow yourself to be persuaded that lenshoods, UV and skylight filters don't belong in the equipment of a real professional.

Circular Polarising Filters

A polarising filter is useful for controlling certain reflections. The filter can be rotated because it will allow the light to pass only in certain directions. This is useful if there are strong reflections from water, windows, gloss paint or plastic surfaces. However, it will not cut-out reflections from metal surfaces. In landscape photography the light from the blue sky at right-angles to the sun is polarized strongly. A polarising filter can be used to darken the blue sky in this direction without affecting the reproduction of other colours. Polarising filters absorb a fair amount of light and you will have to increase the exposure. But this is no problem with the F-401, as the camera will take this into account in all shooting modes. By the way, you will need the more expensive circular polarising filter for the F-401, the cheaper linear polarising filters are unsuitable. The linear filter could interfere with the AF function and produce incorrect focusing.

Be Cautious with Creative Filters

On the matter of creative filters and other attachments, I can only advise you to be cautious. Most of them cannot work as well as the advertisements would have you believe, simply by the laws of physics and optics. Many of these attachments depend on the focal length of the lens, the distance setting, the distance of the filter to the front element, the lighting conditions, etc., etc. One often has to make several exposures with these creative filters and then superimpose them carefully as slides to achieve those picture-book effects. One thing you should remember: good pictures are sometimes better with creative filters, but you will never turn a poor picture into a good one by using such a filter.

A Good Camera Case is Not a Luxury

The use of an ever-ready case, such as Nikon offers in great variety is, in my opinion, not exactly suitable for the photographer. As far as I am concerned such cases are, at best, reasonable protection when I store my camera in a rucksack or in a travel bag. Whenever I wish to take a picture I always find them inconvenient. If you are thinking of accumulating a comprehensive outfit you could save that money and invest in a really good camera bag. Such a bag should be roomy and offer easy access to the equipment. It should also be light and easy to carry, should be spray-proof and reasonably dust-proof, and it should protect your equipment against knocks. As you see, we are expecting a lot of such a bag and this cannot be fulfilled by any cheap old imitation leather bag.

Aluminium cases give the best protection but they are relatively heavy and cumbersome. Just think when you are going on a leisurely walk about town with such a case, particularly if the name NIKON is printed bright and clear on its side, you will soon have to worry more about whether your bag is still at your side, rather than concentrating on some lovely sights. The ideal combination is a good, practical, camera bag which accommodates everything that you need to carry with you (films, spare batteries, set of lenses, dusting brush) and then a transport case for the rest of the equipment.

Stiff, upright leather cases and lens cases are also of limited use. Usually made of the finest leather they look nice but are only useful for storing your expensive lenses. Did you buy your lens to keep them safe in a smart case, or did you want to take pictures? If you want to photograph, you have to have quick access. The best way is to keep your camera, without any case, in the camera bag. However, it is important that the various items carried in the bag do not knock against each other (intermediate compartments). The repeated shocks could cause damage.

Body Cap and Lens Back Cap

One item that is essential is the camera body cap. This should always be on the camera when no lens is fitted. Apart from protection against dust, it prevents your touching the mirror by mistake when you take the camera out of the bag. Once is enough to ruin the surface.

The lens back cap is another essential item. This cap should always be put on as soon as the lens is taken from the camera. Not only could you scratch the back element or leave your fingermarks all over it, but there is also the danger of bending the aperture lever etc. These caps usually fit very badly, even if they are the original Nikon caps, either too loose or hard to fit. Never pull your lens out of the bag by the back cap, unless you want to make some crash tests. You can do without a lens cap for the front of the lens, provided you always use either a UV or a skylight filter.

Service and Care of Your Camera

The care of your F-401 is quite simple. Excessive cleaning will only damage the camera. Any dust that has accumulated in the camera body, for example in the film compartments, has to be removed, otherwise it will adhere to the next film. A dusting brush, or better still a puffer brush, is also suitable for dusting the front and rear elements of the lenses. If you get a fingermark on your lens, it should be removed as soon as possible, because perspiration can attack the lens surface and damage it permanently. Scratches or fingermarks are not directly visible on your photographs, but they will cause them to be noticably low in contrast, as if a bad soft-focus lens had been used. To clean lenses and filters use a lens cleaning tissue and lens cleaning liquid which is obtainable specifically for photographic lenses. Always clean them gently, without exerting any pressure and take care that no dust or hard particles come between the cloth and the lens.

Under no circumstances lubricate your camera or your lenses, not even with the best sewing-machine oil, even if you think something sticks. All cameras and lenses are lubricated when they are assembled, only at those points where it is necessary, which are usually not accessible to you anyway. If you really think your camera makes unusual noises or that the auto-diaphragm is sluggish, then you will have to send it to an appointed dealer to have it examined.

If you take your camera into environments with a lot of dust, or very high humidity, then you will have to keep it in an airtight and waterproof plastic case. If it has to be absolutely waterproof, as say when you take it on a canoe trip, you can get an inflatable bag complete with float. Don't forget that if your camera is kept in such air-tight conditions, condensation can occur and you must not forget to put a porous sachet of drying medium, such as silica gel, into the bag.

In winter, when you bring your camera inside after outdoor

photography, the lens will steam up. The only thing you can do is wipe it gently and leave it standing in the open until it has dried; only then should it be stored away. Better still, leave the camera in the camera bag for some hours until it has warmed up.

One last bit of advice: if you are not using your camera or your flashgun for some time, remove the batteries. Leaking batteries can damage your camera – and four AA size batteries can do a lot of leaking! If you don't use the flashgun for some time you should insert the batteries from time to time. Keep it switched on for a few minutes and then release several times, then re-charge it again and switch it off without discharging it. This procedure will keep the electrolytic capacitor in good condition.

Apart from this you should follow one golden rule. Don't interfere with the camera or the lenses; they don't take kindly to DIY treatment! Always contact your dealer if there are any defects.

Summary of all conventional Nikon lenses and their compatibility with the automatic modes of the F-401

	Exposure facility			Focusing	
	Autofocus	Focus assist	Manual	Automatic	Manual
Zoom lenses					
28～85mm f/3,5～4,5		●	●		●
35～70mm f/3,3～4,5		●	●		●
35～70mm f/3,5		●	●		●
35～105mm f/3,5～4,5		●	●		●
35～135mm f/3,5～4,5		●	●		●
35～200mm f/3,5		●	●		●
50～135mm f/3,5		●	●		●
80～200mm f/2,8 ED		●	●		●
80～200mm f/4		●	●		●
50～300mm f/4,5 ED		●	●		●
100～300mm f/5,6		●	●		●
200～400mm f/4 ED		●	●		●
180～600mm f/8 ED			●		●
Wide-angle lenses					
13mm f/5,6		●	●		●
15mm f/3,5		●	●		●
18mm f/3,5		●	●		●
20mm f/2,8		●	●		●
24mm f/2		●	●		●
24mm f/2,8		●	●		●
28mm f/2		●	●		●
28mm f/2,8		●	●		●
28mm f/3,5		●	●		●
35mm f/1,4		●	●		●
35mm f/2		●	●		●
35mm f/2,8		●	●		●
Standard lenses					
50mm f/1,2		●	●		●
50mm f/1,4		●	●		●
50mm f/1,8		●	●		●
Telephoto lenses					
85mm f/1,4		●	●		●
85mm f/2		●	●		●
105mm f/1,8		●	●		●
105mm f/2,5		●	●		●
135mm f/2		●	●		●
135mm f/2,8		●	●		●
180mm f/2,8 ED		●	●		●
200mm f/2 IF-ED		●	●		●
200mm f/4		●	●		●
300mm f/2 IF-ED		●	●		●
300mm f/2,8 IF-ED		●	●		●
300mm f/4,5		●	●		●

	Exposure facility			Focusing	
	Autofocus	Focus assist	Manual	Automatic	Manual
300mm f/4,5 IF-ED		●	●		●
400mm f/2,8 IF-ED		●	●		●
400mm f/3,5 IF-ED		●	●		●
400mm f/5,6 IF-ED		●	●		●
600mm f/4 IF-ED		●	●		●
600mm f/5,6 IF-ED		●	●		●
800mm f/5,6 IF-ED		●	●		●
800mm f/8 IF-ED			●		●
1200mm f/11 IF-ED			●		●
Mirror lenses					
500mm f/8			●		●
1000mm f/11			●		●
2000mm f/11			●		●
Fisheye lenses					
6mm f/2,8		●	●		●
8mm f/2,8		●	●		●
16mm f/2,8		●	●		●
Specialist lenses					
PC 28mm f/3,5		●	●		●
PC 35mm f/2,8		●	●		●
Noct 58mm f/1,2		●	●		●
Micro 55mm f/2,8		●	●		●
Micro 105mm f/2,8		●	●		●
Micro 200mm f/4 IF		●	●		●
Medical 120mm f/4 IF		●	●		●
UV 105mm f/4,5		●	●		●
AF 80mm f/2,8 (Für F3AF)		●	●		●
AF 200mm f/3,5 IF-ED (Für F3AF)		●	●		●
Series E lenses					
28mm f/2,8		●	●		●
135mm f/2,8		●	●		●

Next page: Nikon AF Lenses for the F-401

Lens	Groups/ elements	Angle of view	Filter dia. (mm)	Lens hood	Weight (g)	Dia. x length (mm)
ZOOM						
24 – 50 mm f/3.3 – 4.5	9/9	84—46°	62	HB-3	375	70,5 × 73,5
28 – 85 mm f/3.5 – 4.5	11/75	74 – 28°	62	HB-1	540	71 × 89
35 – 70 mm f/2.8	12/15	62 – 3°	62	HB-1	665	72 × 95
35 – 70 mm f/3.3 – 4.5	7/8	62 – 34°	52	HN-2	275	70,5 × 61
35 – 105 mm f/3.5 – 4.5	12/16	62 – 32°	52	HB-2	460	69 × 87
35 – 135 mm f3.5/4.5	12/15	62 – 18°	62	HB-1	630	72 × 109
70 – 210 mm f/4.0 – 5.6	12/9	34 – 11°	62	HN-24	590	73,5x108
80 – 200 mm	11/16	30 – 12°	77	HN-28	1200	85.5 × 176.5
WIDE-ANGLE						
24 mm f/2.8	9/9	84°	52	HN-1	260	65 × 46
28 mm f/2.8	5/5	74°	52	HN-2	195	65 × 39
TELEPHOTO						
85 mm f/1.8	6/6	28° 30'	62	HN-23	415	71 × 58,5
180 mm f/2.8 IF-ED	6/8	13° 40'	72	eingebaut	750	78,5 × 144
300 mm f/2.8 IF-ED	6/8	8° 10'	39	eingebaut	2700	133 × 255
300 mm f/4 IF-ED	6/8	8° 10'	39	eingebaut	1330	89 × 211
STANDARD						
50 mm f/1.4	6/7	46°	52	HR-2	255	65 × 42
50 mm f/1.8	5/6	46°	52	HR-2	210	65 × 39
SPECIAL						
Micro 55 mm f 2.8	5/6	43°	62	–	420	74 × 74
AF-TELE CONVERTER TC-16A	5/5	–	–	–	150	69 × 30

Index